Brian Glover: "One of Britain's best-loved

In 2019, as we placed flowers upon Brian Glover's grave in Brompton Cemetery, London, the idea of unveiling a blue plaque in his honour, first came to mind.

Then, three years later, on the 25th anniversary of Brian's death, our group of enthusiasts raised funds and organised the unveiling ceremony in Peel Square and Wellington Street.

The blue plaque was placed outside Chennells Bar where, in the 1970s, Brian was filmed presenting a documentary about his beloved home town of Barnsley.

Most members of the group already knew of Brian's great qualities as a teacher having been taught by him, either at Longcar Central or Racecommon Road Secondary School. They fondly remember his infectious enthusiasm for sport, literature and history but, more importantly, his genuine respect for all his students – rich or poor, male or female.

Moreover, they also sensed that he, like us, had a deep affection for our town and its people.

However, there was obviously much more to Brian Glover, than that. His outstanding achievements as a performer were summed up accurately by the Independent newspaper when it described him, upon his death, as "one of Britain's best-loved actors."

Add to this the 20 short plays and film-scripts he wrote and you realise that Brian Glover's achievements have to be celebrated.

Therefore, Brian Glover - teacher, wrestler, actor, writer and socialist – I am very proud to dedicate to your memory, this, my second book of true tales about growing up in Barnsley.

Ronnie Steele (11/10/2022)

ACKNOWLEDGEMENTS

My heartfelt thanks goes to my partner, Janet Richardson, for her industry and patience when editing this, my second book of true tales. How she puts up with me sometimes, I just don't know?

The following people also deserve huge credit for their invaluable information and advice:

Ged and Barbara Wilcock, Alan and Karen Earp, Lynn Manterfield, John Turner, Richard Hines, Wes Hobson, Rob Rookledge, Mike Bray, Jimmy Ryder, Eva Edgar, Ian Bailey, Milly Johnson and Graham Ibbeson.

If I've missed anyone, which I'm sure to have, may I offer my sincerest apologies.

Ronnie Steele (04/10/2022)

Use of cover-painting granted by kind permission of Barnsley artist, Neil Richardson.

First published in the United Kingdom by Arc Publishing and Print 2022
Copyright © Ronnie Steele 2022

ABOUT THE AUTHOR

Ronnie Steele was born and raised on the Athersley South Council Estate in Barnsley, but at the age of six, his family moved to a terraced house near the centre of town.

He was educated at Agnes Road Junior, Longcar Central and Holgate Grammar School.

His first job was as an apprentice professional footballer; later he worked as a civil servant and finally he spent 28 years as a school teacher in several Barnsley schools.

Ronnie is now a semi professional singer and author and this is his second book containing stories about growing up in Barnsley.

His first book, *Build it for Barry*, was published by Arc Publishing and Print, in 2021, and is regarded as a resounding success.

Ronnie is divorced with two grown up children.

CONTENTS

LEON ARRAS THE MAN FROM PARIS

It's a Saturday afternoon in March 1966 and I'm watching professional wrestling on World of Sport. Wrestling has already been exposed as a sham by several TV documentaries but it doesn't matter one jot because I love to experience the comedy element of it all. The whole purpose is to put on a show, like a pantomime, with goodies and baddies who whip up the emotions. It's comic book stuff.

I'm particularly impressed by commentator, Kent Walton - the voice of professional wrestling. I love to hear his serious tones and always wonder how he manages to maintain an air of solemnity.

The wrestling bout being televised today is between Les Kellet of Bradford and Leon Arras, the man from Paris, who can't speak a word of English. Except, Leon Arris is not who he says he is. He's actually the little-known Brian Glover from Barnsley, who's not yet a household name. He also happens to teach me history and sport at Longcar Central School. Of course, the consummate commentator knows full well that Leon Harris is a fraud, but plays along with the subterfuge.

After one or two sneaky punches by Arras, which the referee and the commentator somehow appear to miss, Kent Walton announces:

"For the spectators here and those viewers at home... I have to say, Leon Arras is not a dirty fighter. He's a foreign gentleman who simply cannot understand the English referee's instructions because, well, he's French."

The ref keeps stopping the fight to tell-off the so called Frenchman but his response is to shrug his shoulders and shake his head.

However, the audience soon smell a rat. Kent and the referee might be easily fooled but *they* aren't. Before the end of Round One, they're on their feet screaming that the Frenchman is a con artist and cheat who's getting away with murder.

As Leon Arras gives a crafty smile and wink to some in the audience, it all gets a bit too much for two old ladies. The camera swings to them as they prepare to enter the ring themselves to mete out their own kind of justice. It's mayhem.

Then the man from Paris raises the temperature by cheating even more, as the ref and Kent continue to maintain their support for the poor "misunderstood" Frenchman. The audience is shouting at the ref and commentator now, not to be so flaming gullible. Surely they can see what a fraud the Frenchman is? What the hell's the matter with them?

Boos ring out for the pantomime villain as he climbs the ropes in the corner, preparing to jump feet first onto the neck of the prostrate Kellet. But out of danger's way, Kellet swiftly rolls and there's a massive cheer as the Frenchman lands awkwardly on the canvas. But now it's Kellet who's throwing the sly punches while his supporters are celebrating wildly. They see this as justifiable revenge. The trickster gets some of his own medicine. "The poor Frenchman is limping badly" says Kent, full of sympathy. "He's hurt!"

I'm fully expecting the audience to shout back. "Oh no he isn't!"

I can see this is not play-acting anymore and what started out as a bit of showmanship has become a lot more serious.

Then the camera shows a close up of the two as Kellet is grabbed fiercely by the throat and the microphone catches the words of the Frenchman who speaks no English:

"If tha does that again, Kellet" he says in a very broad Yorkshire accent "I'll rip thi bloody head off!"

Classic Saturday afternoon wrestling; classic Brian Glover showmanship!

(Many thanks to Mike Kemp for supplying the bones of this tale.)

ONCE BITTEN, TWICE SHY

I'm a very contented infant when I live on Highfield Avenue, Athersley South. We live at number 73 and our newish council home backs on to a large sloping meadow.

Up to the age of four I spend most of my time playing in the back garden. The front and side areas have been nicely cultivated by my dad with the help of our next door neighbour, Mr Davis, because my dad's no gardener.

However, the rear area is just a layer of yellow clay containing a few prickly weeds. In the centre of this is a metal swing, concreted into the ground; and around the swing are a few shallow pot-holes dug by me.

I spend many hours playing on my swing just for the thrill of it and digging holes using my spade that was bought for me in Blackpool. I enjoy sitting at the side of the hole, with my feet resting in the bottom, just loosening the clay and scooping it out. Making deeper and deeper holes gives me an enormous sense of pleasure. I love the feeling of power that shaping my world gives me.

Occasionally, my mam buys me a tiny net-bag filled with half a dozen marbles, which I treasure. I spend hours organising them in rows on the rug in front of the coal fire, hearing them click together and wondering at their sheer beauty. I value them more than anything else apart from my swing and spade.

I become fascinated by number patterns: That four rows of three contains the same number as three rows of four and six rows of two and two of six. I'm thrilled by exploring how to double numbers: Double two is four, double four is eight, double eight is sixteen, and shortly after my sixth birthday I wake up my mam and dad, one Sunday morning, to announce triumphantly that double 256 is 512.

For some reason they don't want to join in my celebrations.

"You'll get 512!" shouts my dad in his tired voice. "It's half past blooming five on a Sunday morning. Get back to sleep." So I conclude that parents are strange creatures. I don't think I'll ever understand them.

I try to wake my sister but she's having none of it, so I dress myself, unlock the side door and sneak out into the back garden to swing and dig.

How can anyone 'lig' in bed when there's a world waiting to be explored?

One evening, later that summer, we hear a commotion in the street and I rush out to see what's happening. On the corner by the cinder path are a dozen teenagers and beside them on the pavement is a homemade wheelbarrow. It's just a wooden box with sloping handles, resting on two old bicycle wheels. The teenagers are launching thousands of brand new marbles down the street and they're rolling past me like pieces of gold begging to be collected. The girls just stand and watch curiously but all the lads are stuffing them in their pockets.

"Ronnie! Ronnie! Get your mam's shopping bag" shouts Trevor Stokes as he picks up a handful and drops them into a peg-bag.

But there's no shopping bag available under our stairs so I pick up an old handbag that my mam's discarded. When I return to the street, a couple of lads have just launched another two full bucket-loads and the whole road is teeming with them.

I click-open the clasp on the handbag and it smells of my mam's old lipstick. Five minutes later, the bag is bulging and I have to drag it up the garden path and in through our front door.

"Nobby Clark says those kids got permission to take the marbles from the glassworks" says my dad as I start to arrange them on the rug.

"And if you believe that you'll believe anything" says my mam, smiling.

My mam is right. There are some rogues on our street who are always up to mischief but they'd all prefer to give a penny than take one. I remember last Mischievous Night watching as the same youths sneakily lifted the Stokes's wrought iron gates off their posts and hid them behind a hedge in next door's garden. Mr Stokes must have had a fit when he found them missing. However, they were soon recovered and no long-term harm was done. It was just a bit of mischief.

My mam throws me some old socks from the sideboard drawer and I start to fill them up with my new windfall. I finish up with ten bulging socks, filled with marbles, which are all identical except for the different coloured centres. I keep them in a cardboard box under the stairs.

From that day forward, playing marbles on our street becomes an even bigger craze than usual and because we're on a council estate there's always lots of kids my own age to play with.

'Follows' is a popular marbles game but 'Podge' is easily my favourite. A podge is a very shallow hole scoured out of the ground and this is how you play the game:

Two competing players decide how many 'mabs' they're gambling with. It might be two each or they could even go up to twelve each. A game of twelve each is called a "Twenty-fourer". Then each player drops their mabs over the podge and the person who gets the most marbles in it, starts. When it's your turn you try and nudge the marbles into the podge one at a time. If you roll too hard it might run in and then pop out the other side – too gently and it'll stop short. When you miss the podge it's your opponent's turn. The person who sinks the very last marble wins the lot.

It's a wonderfully exciting game when you win. But as a six-year old, if you lose a twenty-fourer, your heart sinks into your boots.

All the other lads are older and a bit more experienced, so I don't gamble more than two marbles at a time with them.

One week in the summer of 1960, Trevor Stokes wants to play me in a twenty-fourer and although I really can't afford to lose, the very thought of lifting twenty-four out of the podge is very tempting. After humming and harring for ages, greed gets the better of me and I decide to give it a go.

My mam and dad see me counting my gambling stake into a grey school sock.

Outside, the word soon spreads that a big game is in the offing and lots of kids turn up to watch. Mick Stead sits on his trolley observing; Don Trainer stands with his bike leaning against the privet hedge; Graham Day turns up to see how skilful we are and Les Holt is observing from the kerb. There's also Shirley Stokes and Don's younger sister, Valerie, watching from a short distance. The actual podge is on the pavement where a depression has been scoured out by a shoe heel or two. The ground is dry and dusty.

Soon the game begins in earnest and after 15 minutes the podge is filled with 22 glass balls and only two are left to be sunk.

It's my turn.

The first one's a sitter and easily converted, but the second one is about three strides away from the hollow. I'm so nervous I feel sick to the stomach. There's silence except for a distant motor-cycle engine. I take up position on one knee and present the first finger of my left hand to the last marble. Unfortunately, my arm suddenly feels all weak. I start to picture it not even reaching the podge. My body begins to tremble slightly but I'm still okay. I can do this.

Here goes.

"Look at his hand, it's shaking" shouts Don Trainer and I'm put off completely. Instead of waiting for my confidence to return I just want to get it over with, so I nudge the final marble forward without proper care. It runs nicely over the rough ground towards the hollow but, as it joins the others in the podge, it forces one marble to pop out at the other side.

"Aw!" cry the spectators in disbelief. And all Trevor has to do is to nudge in the last marble to win the game and lift his winnings.

I've lost and I'm feeling a terrible pain in my stomach. It's a devastating blow.

So this is what it feels like to be a big loser.

Oh no! Then I experience the ultimate ignominy as my eyes fill up with tears. I desperately hope no one notices. "Boys don't cry" is something that's been drilled into us all from birth. I walk home alone, carrying my limp sock.

"You're quiet. Is something wrong?" asks my mam.

"No, no, I'm okay" I say, trying my best to smile but failing miserably. There's no fooling my mam.

I'm only six years old but the lesson I learn on this dreadful summer's day is one that lasts me a lifetime. I still adore the excitement of taking risks but never when the forfeit is a large amount of money or anything else I value highly.

In September, 1960, we move three miles to a new house. I occasionally bump into some of my old Athersley friends and it feels good when I hear about their many successes but there are others that I never see or hear of again.

Twenty years later I read in the Barnsley Chronicle that Trevor Stokes's father becomes the boss of ICI UK – one of the biggest multinational companies in the world. Now that's not bad for someone from a council estate.

In fact, having been brought up on Athersley South I would say, with conviction, that people from places like our estate are vastly under-rated people in every way.

Update: Later on in my young life I love playing board games like Monopoly because the gains and losses are only imaginary. However, losing the

"Twenty-fourer" to Trevor does have a lasting effect on me – steering me permanently away from proper gambling.

Could a win against Trevor on that memorable summer's day, have pushed me in the opposite direction? Perhaps. But as far as I'm concerned it was a matter of "once bitten, twice shy".

* Spice. A local word meaning 'sweets'.

THE (NOT SO) GOOD OLD DAYS

It's the Autumn Term of 1962 and I'm an eight year old pupil at Agnes Road Junior School for Boys. This morning I have an appointment at New Street Clinic for an eyesight test.

Going to the clinic is a regular thing for all Barnsley youngsters, which I don't mind, really. At least you escape school for an hour or two.

On first entering the building you can smell the ether, like the Victory V lozenges you buy from the chemist's to clear a blocked nose. I adore it and I wish I could breathe it in all day.

In the central waiting room is a wooden slide and I spend the waiting time playing on it with two other kids. When I reach the bottom I race back to the steps as fast as I can, overtaking the slowcoaches.

After about ten minutes we're called into a room where a middle-aged nurse sits filling in a form. Oh no! It's Nurse Lindley. She's horrible and she's the one thing that puts me off the clinic. Without ever smiling she always talks to you like you're already guilty of doing something wicked. I think she hates kids and worse still, she's got cross-eyes and wears jam-jar bottomed glasses.

"Name?" she demands, and when I look up to answer, she's one eye focussed on my mam and one on me, so I remain silent.

"His name is Ro..."

"Let the boy speak for himself" interrupts Nurse Lindley

I can see my mam's not at all happy with the way she's been spoken to, but Nurse Lindley seems to talk to everyone like that - except when she has to converse with the doctor or dentist.

"R-r-ronnie" I say, nervously.

"And has Ronald got a surname, by any chance?" she asks sarcastically.

I look at my mam for help. I've no idea what my 'sir name' is.

My mam bangs her handbag down on the little coffee table beside her and says, "Nurse Lindley, isn't his surname written on the record card in front of you?"

Nurse Lindley looks surprised that she's met resistance. "Yes, Mrs Steele, but what *you people* don't realise is that we have to double check names and birthdates so we don't accidentally treat the wrong person. It's part of our intensive training."

"*You people?*" repeats my mam, aghast. "And is it part of your intensive training to talk to a child as if he's a dog?" says my mam.

"Mrs Steele, there's no need to be rude!"

"Respect is a two-way street, Nurse Lindley."

Good old mam. And I picture my mam turning into Popeye, swallowing a tinful of spinach and smashing Nurse Lindley through the wall. I look across to my mam and I can tell she's still very cross. No one bullies her. Her face has gone white and she's starts to blink fast – a sure sign she's about to explode.

You'd better be careful, Nurse Lindley.

Nurse Lindley's voice softens as she puts drops into my eyes but she still tuts when I blink. Then she weighs and measures me, writing the data on my record card.

After that, she takes us to another row of seats in the corridor where we wait to see the optician. Ten minutes later, Nurse Lindley invites us into the optician's room and she suddenly becomes 'all sweetness and light'. I notice how she giggles like a nervous school girl now she's in the presence of the optician.

When all the tests are complete we leave the building and I hear my mam saying to herself,

"Edna bloody Lindley. Who does she think she is? She was only brought up on the Barebones like us, and I remember her family didn't have a pot to pee in. Fancy, her saying, *'you people'*."

As we walk through the pile of windswept leaves outside the main doors, my mam gives me a letter for my teacher.

"Whatever you do, love, don't forget to give this letter to Miss Fish" she says" spitting on her palm and patting down a few disobedient sticky-up hairs near my crown.

It's playtime and all my mates are chasing round the playground, so I soon join them and forget about the letter completely.

Back in the classroom Miss Fish has arranged the chairs differently. She tells us we are to have a number test and we mustn't copy answers off our neighbour. Miss Fish detests copycats. When she tells us to open the little booklet in front of us, I find the writing is really strange. The numbers are fuzzy and I can't tell the difference between 3 and 8 or 1 and 7 or 5 and 6. I look across at Barry Thornton's booklet and the writing's just as blurred.

"Ronald Steele!" shouts Miss Fish. Stop trying to cheat!" and I feel her hand slap the back of my head. Ouch! That stings! but I'm not sure what I hate most, being called Ronald or feeling the burn from the slap.

After half an hour, everyone's finished except me. Then I remember my letter and hand it to Miss Fish, and for some reason she's furious and calls me a blockhead!

"Ronald Steele, you're a blockhead. What are you?"

"A blockhead, Miss."

After lunch Miss Fish hands the booklets back to us and I only have three correct out of 60. However, the fuzzy numbers have returned to near-normal by now and I'm shocked at how babyish my writing is. Was it the eyes-drops that caused this?

Then Miss Fish explains that the person who got all his sums correct, will sit at the front of Row One. "Well done, John" she says "you're top of the class" and then she instructs us all to applaud him. It's strange but that makes me dislike John even though he's a friend. The word 'jealous' is not yet part of my lexicon but it's certainly something I feel. Miss Fish is wearing a friendly smile when allocating the top places but this changes to contempt when she's dealing with the bottom row. Soon, there's only one remaining place and I'm the only one standing. I finish up at the very back of the fourth row – number 36 out of a possible 36. And if my classmates do forget who's the dimmest in the room, they only have to look around. Then I also notice that none of us in the bottom row is wearing a school uniform but everyone in the top row is.

Miss Fish then announces that this is where we'll continue to sit every day until the end of the school year.

What? Every blooming day? That's not right! But there's nothing I can do. I want to tell my mam all about it. She'd soon sort it, but I fear she'll be more annoyed with me for forgetting to give my teacher the letter straight away, so I keep it bottled up.

I'm only eight years old but it's been made perfectly clear that learning in class is treated just like a running race. Those who do well are cheered and those who do badly are humiliated. We duffers are not actually booed, but we might as well be and we're bright enough to realise, even at such a tender age, that this is a crude trick used to make us all try harder. It might possibly work to some extent because who wants to be labelled 'bottom'? On the other hand it creates petty jealousy and friction: Your mates become your competitor; some of your friends become your enemy.

I consider making a case to Miss Fish to move places but she keeps a rounders bat beside her desk for when she's upset. I've seen her smack kids really hard on the backside just for being noisy or biting their pencil. However, funnily enough, I notice she never seems to smack anyone from the top row and I conclude this is because these kids are superior in every way to the rest of us.

Even after many months, I still can't work out why we, at the lower end of the class, are considered less worthy. However, one day something happens which helps me make sense of it all.

It's the start of the Summer Term and Miss Fish begins a new topic on coal mining. She asks those whose father works at the pit, to raise their hands. I feel fairly certain that mine will be the only hand to go up but I'm shocked and feel an odd sense of collective pride when a forest of hands are raised. Almost all those in the second, third and fourth rows have their hands in the air. That's most of the class. However, not one hand is raised in the top row. Not one. This gets my nine year old brain working over-time.

Why don't their dads work at the pit? Where do they work? Is that why Miss Fish likes them, because their dads aren't miners? I look at the kids in the top row and though I couldn't tell you exactly what all their fathers do for a living, I do know about quite a few. There's the son of an architect, the son of an optician and three others whose parents own small to large-sized shops. Moreover, the other outstanding thing they all have in common, is that they talk posh compared to the rest of us.

So I get the feeling that Miss Fish prefers children who talk posh, wear school uniform, and have a dad who is NOT a miner.

As the summer term progresses I begin to notice that all those in the top row are offered further privileges that none of the rest of us receive. They're allowed for example, to make the tea for the staff just before break time. Again, I'm envious. Furthermore, during music lessons, the top-row kids are given all the more sophisticated instruments and complex parts to play. The rest of us are given a triangle which you have to ting perhaps once during a whole piece of music. If I was braver I'd ting in the wrong place just to be awkward.

It's humiliating but there's nothing I can do except harbour growing resentment.

What a huge pity this is, because Miss Fish is an otherwise gifted teacher. In fact, despite her snobbery, I learn absolutely loads that school year, especially in History, Science and Scripture. Moreover, it's vital that I don't tar all those who deal with kids, with the same brush. Our head teacher, Mr Rushforth, treats everyone with respect and Mr Parker who sometimes fills in for Miss Fish, is a lovely kind man. Furthermore, it would be very wrong to assume all nurses are nasty like Nurse Lindley. It's just that, in truth, during the 1950s and 60s, there are too many people in authority who are hostile to children, especially those from the working class - as if kids will take advantage of their kindness and end up in prison, unless you come down on them hard.

The year does end on a high note. I work hard in preparation for the end-of-year tests and do quite well. The result is, I'm placed in the second row for the last couple of weeks of term. However, I still feel sorry for those who continue to linger at the bottom. It's a mark of shame.

New Street Clinic

Despite this turn-up in fortunes, my final school report is disappointing because Miss Fish seems to find it hard to write anything more encouraging than 'Fair'- whatever that means. My mam says it means 'okay' and the effect this has on me is to wonder whether trying my best in school is a total waste of effort.

THE CHURCH MONEY-SPINNER

From the age of five I do my best to find different ways of making a little extra pocket money. My parents don't actually encourage me in this but they don't actively discourage me either.

It's 1959 and in October and early November we have kids, usually brothers and sisters, knocking on our door asking for a 'penny for the guy'. My parents are quite generous but not if you come to our door more than once.

"Penny for the guy, eh?" says my dad, remembering all the kids' faces and examining the effigy in the homemade wheelbarrow.

"Aye, it's a well-made guy, I'll give you that, so it's worth a few pence. Well done kids."

This sounds to me like a smart way of making a bit of extra cash.

At Xmas, we hear children singing carols at our door for a few coppers, and by December 1960, I give it a try myself along with my mate, Rob Rookledge.

Sometimes we're chased out of gardens by vicious guard dogs or we spend five minutes singing five verses of We Three Kings, only to hear someone shouting at the end of it:

"You're too early. Come back on Xmas Eve!"

Three years later, in November 1963, both Rob and I are living in neighbouring streets in the centre of Barnsley. Now we're singing carols and making money from those who live in terraced houses off Racecommon Road. My mam says we shouldn't start carolling until December but we give it a go anyway, with moderate success.

One smoggy evening in late November, Rob can't make it, so I pair-up with Glyn Morris. Rob and I are pretty decent singers but Glyn can sing like an angel. Someone, from almost every house we visit stops watching telly, comes to the door to listen, praises Glyn, and fills our money bag with coppers. That evening, Glyn and I share our earnings at their kitchen table. We make the magnificent sum of two shillings and nine pence ha'penny, each!

"Hey, you're not a bad singer you know, Ronnie. Why don't you join St Edward's Church choir? Me and our Gareth are members" says Glyn in his high-pitched voice.

"Church? Me? I don't think so, Glyn. I had enough of Sunshine Corner when I lived up Athersley."

"I bet you'd really enjoy it and we're short of good singers. Why don't you give it a try?"

"No. It's not for me, Glyn. It's not much fun having to be 'good' all the time" I reply.

"We *do* have some fun" he persists.

"Thanks, but no thanks, Glyn. I'm really not bothered."

Then slowly and very deliberately he says, "We-get-paid-five-bob-for-weddings."

There's a pause.

"Well why didn't you say that in the first place? That changes everything. Five bob, eh? Hmm..."

"Yep, five bob and we've got a wedding coming up this Saturday morning, an' all" says Glyn. "Of course I'll have to miss the morning matinee at the Ritz but..."

I stare into space thinking about what I could spend five shillings on.

"That's a lot of money, Glyn. It only costs me a shilling* at Finney's for four penn'orth of chips, two penn'orth of peas, a sausage-in-batter and a bottle of pop. I could treat myself to that five times with five bob!"

"Or you could spend it on something more sensible" says Glyn. Oh, and by the way, you're also expected to go to choir practise every Friday and attend either morning or evening services on Sundays."

On Friday 22nd November I turn up at the vestry and I'm introduced to the choirmaster, Mr Rowlands, and the pianist, Mrs Sugden. They take my details and we spend an hour rehearsing songs for the Saturday wedding and Sunday service. Mrs Sugden gets me kitted out in blue tunic, white cassock and pleated ruff.

That evening, as I walk down Racecommon Road on my way home, I bump into my mate, Carl Ashton.

"Ey up, Ronnie. Have you heard the news?" he says.

"What news?"

"President Kennedy's been shot dead."

I'm stunned.

I'm only nine years old but the media has done a great job in convincing me President Kennedy is a superstar –almost on a par with Rocketman and Batman. I feel genuine shock and grief for a man who lives thousands of miles away, whom I've never met.

That night there's wall-to-wall coverage on both TV channels. The whole of the western world is in mourning. Lee Harvey Oswald is arrested but he's shouting at the TV cameras, claiming he's 'a patsy'. I work out that a patsy is someone who's blamed for something they haven't done and I immediately wonder whether he's been set-up. It's all so shocking but at the same time, exciting.

That night, before I go to sleep, I have a go at this 'praying lark'. I know God can perform magic because I've heard about him turning water into wine and healing the lame, so they can walk:

"Dear God. As you probably know I've always wanted an electric-train set and never got one. I know now that there's no such thing as Father Christmas so I'm putting all my hopes in you. It would be lovely if, when I look under my bed in the morning, the train-set is there waiting for me.

Love you,

Amen."

I feel certain the 'Love-you' bit will swing it. But something goes wrong because when I look under my bed next morning, all I see is fluff.

In the vestry, Mr Rowlands says we must forget about the assassination and make sure that the couple getting married have a joyous ceremony.

All ten choir boys walk up the steps from the vestry and into the church. Imagine my surprise when, on entering the main part of the church for the first time, I see my 'Sunday' name on a brass plaque.

RONALD STEELE

I do a double take and can't take my eyes off it. Is this God's response to last night's prayer? As our procession of choirboys stops for a moment in front of the altar, I bump into Steve Evans in front of me, and almost cause a pile up.

We're told to assemble on the benches, which in the church are called 'pews'' It's a good job Rob Rookledge is not here because he would be sure to have me giggling at that unfortunate name. There are five choirboys sitting in each pew, as Mr Rowlands plays soft sombre background music on the church organ.

Suddenly, he raises the volume and bangs out, *Here Comes the Bride* and we all have to stand. From that time until the end of the ceremony I'm trying to make sense of why my name's displayed on a brass plaque for all to see.

Spending time in church makes me think about God and religion. I remember my teacher telling me that God knows absolutely everything – even what you're thinking; and I begin to wonder if this God-fellow has put my name on the brass plaque because he knows I'm a fraud and I'm only here for the five bob.

Gulp!

The sound of the *Wedding March* wakes me from my reverie and as I look all around, everyone's smiling and happy for the bride and groom.

Outside church, with my five shillings in my pocket, I confide in Glyn that this is the first and last time that I'll be singing in the choir. I tell him I feel rotten for pretending to be all good and angelic when I'm only interested in the money. I also mention my name on the brass plaque.

Glyn laughs out loud and says,

"They're just the names of people in the parish who died in the war, you ninny."

"Ah, I see. Yes, my Uncle Ron died in World War II. Whooo! That's a relief, Glyn" I tell him, and I start to smile.

"Don't feel too bad about going for the money. Me and our Gareth wouldn't refuse it" he replies. "Anyway, you need to put your name down for the pantomime in Sheffield in January. It's free; and next summer there's the wine and cheese party under a big marquee and you can get a drink when no one's looking. We all did last year."

I'm feeling tempted. It's not fair that only adults are allowed to do exciting things.

Two days later there's more drama on our TV screens. Lee Harvey Oswald is shot dead by a vigilante called Jack Ruby. The shooting is caught on camera for the whole world to see.

For the second time in 48 hours the people of the world, who have access to TV or radio, are knocked sideways.

"How very convenient" says my dad, and I think I know exactly what he means. I'm only at junior school but even I can see that there's something very fishy about the events surrounding the assassination of John F Kennedy and now, Lee Harvey Oswald.

After a bit of time to reflect, I decide to carry on as a choirboy, even though my face doesn't seem to fit with Mr Rowlands. He's not actually hostile towards me but I always get the impression that he doesn't particularly like me. Maybe he's sussed me out for my deceit. I don't know.

The visit to the panto at the Sheffield Lyceum is the best live show I've ever seen. I've watched Peter Goodwright before, on TV, but never thought he was as funny as he is live.

Even though I continue with Friday choir practice and the services on Sunday, they are incredibly boring and I occupy my mind by day-dreaming, looking round at the architecture and stained glass windows, reading the signs or notices and looking through the hymn book.

Some of the hymns are great though. I absolutely love, *Now Thank We All Our God* and *Thine is the Glory,* but I detest, with a passion, the foul smell of the candles when they're snuffed out. I consider putting in an official complaint but think better of it.

In June 1964 we're asked to collect dirty plates and wine glasses at the wine and cheese party, in the vicarage garden.

Mr Rowlands is no fool but he can't understand our response.

That Friday all twelve regular choir boys turn up for practice plus Rob Rookledge and one other newcomer.

Mr Rowlands asks:

"We need some helpers to collect dirty plates and..."

Fourteen hands shoot up into the air.

"Hang on a minute" he says. "You don't even know what you're volunteering for. I need 10 boys for tomorrow to collect dirty plates and glasses and take them to the vicarage for washing and return them to the marquee for re-use."

Again, all 14 choirboys raise an arm showing their keenness to volunteer.

Mr Rowlands is pleased but puzzled. He and Mrs Sugden look at each other and shrug their shoulders to show they can't make sense of this extraordinary enthusiasm for work.

"Okay then" he says. All 14 of you can help out tomorrow but I'm going to have to reduce your fee from half-a-crown each, to two-shillings. But you must turn up clean and smart and behave with politeness. What do you all say to that?"

I open my mouth and say,

"I didn't even know we were getting paid for..." and I feel a nudge in my back from Steve Evans who's trying to tell me to shut up.

Next day, we all turn up on time, looking like Bobby Dazzlers. There must be 30 to 40 adult parishioners there, but none of them come from round our way. They're all wealthy people with posh accents. I can't imagine any of them playing bingo in Kingstone Club or emerging from the bookies on Racecommon Road with a folded newspaper, smoking a Woodbine.

After half an hour, wine glasses are left on the cloth-covered tables while the party-goers try a different vintage. The empties are taken back to the vicarage, two at a time, and between the marquee and the house, the dregs are downed by the angels with scrubbed-up faces.

First, I try a morsel of cheese that's been left. Yuk! I've never tasted anything as vile. It's got blue veins and it smells just like sweaty socks. I spit it out into a bin and thank goodness, no one's watching. There's an inch of dark red wine that's been left. I've never tasted wine before but it smells delightful, so I knock it back as fast as I can to get rid of the taste of cheese. Argh! It's like drinking pure vinegar. I walk out of the tent and round the back to spit out what's coated my tongue.

The strange thing is, a few minutes later, my senses have got used to the wine-taste and now I find the tang is quite pleasant.

By late afternoon it's not just the posh parishioners who are tipsy.

That autumn we're asked if we'd like to attend confirmation classes in order to become confirmed Christians. I've always fancied tasting the 'blessed' wine from the golden chalice, and that wafer the vicar feeds you also looks rather tasty, so I give it a go.

For another 12 months I carry on going to church, sipping the wine, collecting my five-shilling wedding-fee and being bored. However, in the end, what really convinces me to pack-in is the unease I feel about religion.

At eleven years old I want a serious conversation with a deep-rooted believer who will not be offended if I ask questions like:

Have you ever actually seen God or Jesus?

Do you think that believing in God protects you from bad things happening to you?

What happens to people after they die?

Have you ever wondered whether the idea of God is just made up?

And what if all this church business is a massive waste of time and money?

In the end I find I'm not at all convinced about religion. Serious doubts had set in early doors when God didn't respond to my train-set prayer. That was God's chance of winning over my support and that of all my mates. He'd have done much better with me singing his praises. Nevertheless, I certainly don't regret my 18 months or so, as a choirboy at St Edward's. I learnt a lot and the extra pocket money came in very handy.

Anyway, soon I'll be getting a paper-round, and me, Rob Rookledge and Barry Thornton are also going to get a job during the school holidays. We've heard Beckett's pop factory on Shaw Lane is expanding.

* An old shilling is worth the same as a modern five-pence piece, when we go metric.

A bob is the slang word for shilling.

There were 12 old pence in one shilling.

(This story is written as a tribute to my old friend, Glyn Morris, 1954 – 2020 and his brother, Gareth, 1956 - 1975)

LOSING GIVES ME WINGS

I'm a terrible loser no matter what I play - football, cricket, snooker, darts, musical chairs, marbles, Monopoly, running, fighting, anything. I just can't help it and I'm convinced it's instinctive. Fish love swimming, birds love flying, I love winning.

I play, I win, I rejoice;

I play, I lose, I lament...

And it literally takes me hours before I can get over failure and feel a twinge of pleasure. Occasionally, when I'm at my worst, I've been known to cheat, bully or even fight, in order to win... and then find unconvincing ways to justify my loutishness.

I haven't a clue what's made me like this. After all, my friends love to compete and although they prefer winning to losing, they can still accept defeat and get pleasure from the game. Nor can I lay the blame at the door of my parents or teachers, because they all insist on competitors being "good losers". Unfortunately, the very sound of this phrase sets my teeth on edge like squeaky chalk on a blackboard.

So I find it impossible to accept advice from wiser people to shake hands in defeat, like a gentleman, and shout "Three cheers for the winners!"

Perhaps surprisingly, this attitude doesn't make me unpopular. Most people my own age afford me a certain respect for my never-say-die attitude. They seem to like the passion that drives me to stretch every sinew in order to succeed.

During the summer of 1964, Ian Bailey and I are picked for our school to compete in the Barnsley Schools' Swimming Gala at Race Street Baths. There's about ten in our team and most of us are only third year students.

My best swimming stroke is front crawl so I'm eager to take part in this competition. However, our captain Ian Bailey, is easily the best in school, so he and Charlie Barham are selected. I finish up being dragooned into entering for the backstroke competition.

"You two are volunteering for the 25 metres backstroke race" says Mr Bates, looking meaningfully at me and Steve Wathey. Steve is good at backstroke but I'm useless. Yes, I could swim a mile doing it, but this race is a sprint not a marathon.

"And you can get that sour look off your face, Ronnie Steele. The team comes first, don't forget" says Mr Bates, taking a long draw on his filter tipped cigarette, followed by a prolonged coughing fit.

"Come on Ronnie, I'll let you take my place in the diving competition if you do" says my mate, Rob Rookledge.

That's the clincher for me. I love diving because I know I'm decent at it.

"Yes, Mr Bates, backstroke and diving for me, please" I tell him, as I send Rob the thumbs-up as a thank you.

Mr Bates goes into another bout of coughing as he re-jigs the entrance form.

*   *   *   *   *   *   *   *   *

Race Street swimming pool area is packed with noisy spectators when we're called to line up for the 25 metre backstroke event. There are four tiers of adult spectators squashed into both sides of the pool area. The very front row is so close to the water they could almost dangle their feet in it. There's a plastic anti-splash apron to protect them, held up by a thick rope.

The announcer, who is hidden from view, says over the tannoy:

"Heat One of the 25 metres backstroke competition" and as he calls out the name of each school there's a huge cheer from their supporters.

Lane One: Keir Street.

Lane Two: St Edwin's.

Lane Three: Agnes Road. (I wave to our supporters, particularly my mam, dad and sister)

Lane Four: St Mary's.

Lane 5: Doncaster Road.

I'm not looking forward to this. The butterflies in my stomach have gone into panic mode. We're then told to jump into the shallow end and take our marks, get set and go... on the whistle's piercing blast.

I'm off to a flier but before we reach halfway I'm already at the back. When my ears dip below the surface, all the noise disappears but the cheering is deafening when they're above water. The chlorine-filled splashes get into my eyes and nostrils. I look at the moving ceiling and then at the supporters at the side and realise I'm lagging well behind. At the three-quarter mark, the cheering has stopped because the rest have already finished. I can see spectators looking at me, laughing and waving me forward. Worse still, when I reach the finish I receive an extra special applause for being a good sport, which makes things ten times worse. I've now become an object of fun and I detest it. An infant points me out to her mam and shouts,

"He's wubbish, him!"

The fact that my performance is summed up so accurately by a child so young, makes my humiliation ten times worse.

However, rather than sulk and entertain the idea of dropping out altogether, I feel a burning passion welling up from the very top of my head down to the tips of my fingers and toes. I've now got, what I call, "my mad up" and I'm already looking for redemption. Nobody had better cross me.

Apart from my ignominious performance that day, Agnes Road actually does brilliantly. After each race the scores are updated on a blackboard and we're neck and neck with St Edwins for the lead, with only two events to follow - the 4 x 50 yards medley relay and the diving competition. If we can win the relay we can't be caught - but things get off to a terrible start. We're well behind the others. However, on the final leg, we have Ian Bailey so there's still hope. He's no chance of winning because we're more than half a length down, but if Ian can come second, then Agnes Road are in with a chance of overall victory. By the time he enters the water we're in last place with the St Edwin's lad miles in front but tiring. Ian swims crawl with his back and shoulders sticking out of the water like a speedboat, and is in second place at the turn and gaining. The noise of the crowd, amplified by the hall's acoustics, is raised to a roar, and I can see our head teacher, Mr Rushforth, standing by the scoreboard with a stick of chalk in his hand shouting at the top of his lungs:

"Come on Bailey! Come on lad! You can do it" and Mr Rushforth's body is bent forward and his arms and shoulders are moving like he's actually swimming the race himself. And as the leaders touch the finishing wall it's unclear, from where I stand, who finishes first, but I've no need to wait for an official announcement. My mam and dad and sister, plus Ian's mam and dad are positioned in line with the finish and they're on their feet jumping about and celebrating. So it's all over now. We've won the race, and won the day, no matter what happens in the diving competition.

However, personal redemption is now my top priority.

"Will the contestants for the diving competition please assemble on the bath-side at the deep end?" says the hidden voice. As soon as I hear this the world seems to change around me. Everything goes into slow motion and all sounds become a distant echo. I have no control over my thoughts and the voice in my head says, "You're going to win this, Ronnie Steele. Nothing can possibly stop you, mate. You'll show 'em. Then we'll see who's rubbish."

We tread carefully from the bath-side at the shallow end, up a narrow corridor between the blue splash-sheet and the pool, towards the deep end. When I draw level with my family I'm feeling supremely determined and confident.

"I'm going to win this" I say to them as I pass, as though I've already watched the event on TV and I know the result. It's not a feeling of over-confidence; it's more one of nothing-can-possibly-stop-me. Normally I'd be reminding myself of all the dos and don'ts about diving, but nothing as negative as that crosses my mind.

The actual aim for the diving contestants is to enter the water vertically and create as little splash as possible. If you can do that and keep your fingers and toes neat, you can't fail.

My first dive is spot on and only when I come up to the surface do I hear the fantastic cheering of our supporters. I'm still swimming neatly as I head for the steps in the corner of the pool and I feel my trunks have slipped down, but not noticeably.

I'm in the final with four others and as I score top marks I get to do my final dive, last.

My brain enters lockdown again where all is silent and I see people around me moving, as if in slow motion.

Now it's time for my final dive. I walk up smartly to the edge of the deep end.

I pause.

I raise both arms above my head making sure my fingers are together and my thumbs are touching.

I stand on tiptoes and with a little spring, dive towards the smooth surface of the water.

As I touch the bottom of the pool I know for sure that my dive is perfect. Somehow you can always tell, and when I reach the surface, I swim towards the steps and hear our supporters whistling and cheering. Even the parents of the losers recognise my perfect dive merits the top possible score and applaud politely. I make sure I carefully hitch my trunks up again to save my blushes.

The sights and sounds of the baths have now returned to normal.

"In first place, Steele, Agnes Road Junior School for Boys" says the nasal voice over the tannoy and I march over to the Mayor who offers a handshake and presents me with the winner's medal – my first medal ever.

The rest of the Aggy Road team gather at the place where I'm standing, to be announced as Barnsley Schools' Champions.

Ian, still wearing his trunks and with a bath towel round his shoulders, says, "I knew you'd win it, Steelie. And Rob Rookledge, already changed, says with a huge grin, "I deserve a share of that medal."

Mr Rushforth announces that he's proud of us all and that we must remember to bring our trunks to school on Tuesday so that the Chronicle photographer can take a team picture.

The weird thing is, the odd events of that day are not the first time this has happened, nor is it the last. In fact it starts to become a fairly regular occurrence.

However, I do fully accept that normally such extreme emotions get in the way of a good performance, but like the father who single-handedly lifts a car off the injured body of his son, these extreme emotions sometimes give us greater powers, not less.

For me, personally, I love the benefits that being a rotten loser, brings.

BONFIRE NIGHT IN DAYS GONE BY (1964)

There are no big community bonfires in Barnsley during the 1950s and early 60s. Families, or small groups of neighbours, organise their own.

Bonfire Night is a hands-on experience and not just an event for spectators. Everyone has a role to play in making it a success, except perhaps the very old and very young. We, as school kids, create crude effigies of Guy Fawkes and ask passers-by to donate a penny-for-the-Guy. This is usually used to buy our own fireworks which we often detonate ourselves on the big day, at considerable risk.

All the people who live in the dozen or so houses in our terraced row come together each year to savour the evening. The tradition has been identical since my father was a child: It isn't planned, no invitations are issued, nobody's expected to bring something to the party but nearly everybody does.

While we're at school all our neighbours bring out their inflammable rubbish and dump it for incineration just outside our back garden gate -between the fence and the outbuildings. The wigwam-shaped structure consists of combustible household and garden waste, including a pair of massive, white knickers. And right at the summit of the pile, looking rather precarious, sitting astride a wobbly chair, is my bearded Guy Fawkes. There's also a load of spare fuel to replenish the fire as it dies back. All this is stored in a heap on the neglected rockery, nearby.

An old two-seater sofa and four discarded dining room chairs are strategically placed so our elderly neighbours can have a comfortable, ring-side seat, until it's time that is, to commit the furniture to the flames.

By 5 o'clock, it's pitch black outside and me, my older sister, Pauline, and Rob Rookledge, are following my dad to the bonfire pile with lots of newspapers to stuff inside the conical structure. It's windy so we have to make sure the sticks of newspaper are not allowed to blow away.

In the distance, an early rocket whistles into the lonely night and explodes, showering golden sparks over St Edward's Parish Church. Some people, on nearby streets, have started their fires early and the odour of burnt wood is wafting our way. We're impatient for the fire to start but my dad's concerned about his garden fence and outhouse doors getting scorched like they did last year. He hands me and Rob a galvanised bucket each.

"Fill 'em up at the outside tap and rinse the fence and coalhouse doors to protect them from t'fire" he says, whilst taking a drag on his cigarette. The end glows bright red like a traffic light and although I can hardly see my dad, I can still trace his movements.

I try to drench the wooden fence but my right hand slips off the bottom of the bucket and most of the water goes all over me. My sister thinks it's hilarious and my dad calls me a "reight tea cake" as I go back into the house to change. My old jeans are on the Guy so I have to wear my new school trousers.

In our kitchen my mam has scrubbed a score of jacket spuds and put them in the oven. Already they're giving off their delightful smell. Two huge pans of mushy peas are also bubbling away on the gas rings.

I'm changed in a jiffy and back outside to hear a big cheer from further up the street. The Sugdens are just lighting their conflagration. Why isn't ours burning? In the distance more fireworks are crackling and the two poor dogs that are always roaming around our backyard are trembling at home in their baskets, whimpering at the TV.

Soon a dozen people of all ages are crowding round the wigwam, chatting and laughing. So dad wraps a piece of paraffin-soaked rag around a stick and lights it with a match. He then broddles it into the heart of the structure until every part of it catches light. In a couple of minutes the yellow flames are licking the dry wood and illuminating the faces of the encircling audience.

Our bonfire party is always the best in the street, so lots of teenagers in the neighbourhood, each with a bag of fireworks, gatecrash it. They're all mischievous lads and lasses but there's never any bother and everyone's made to feel very welcome.

Suddenly, a massive cheer erupts and when I look round I see the leg of my Guy Fawkes has bursts into flames. There goes my old jeans and snake belt. Old Mrs Gledhill and Edith Freeman, sit comfortably on the sofa, both faces reddening. The strong wind keeps swirling round, occasionally blowing the acrid smoke into unprotected eyes and nostrils. A burning wooden pit-prop collapses into the centre of the fire and ten thousand wild sparks billow upwards into the night sky. As the fire gets hotter everyone has to withdraw, including those elderly folk on the chairs.

When the Ashworth family appear, a big cheer can be heard because Mrs Ashworth makes superb toffee and there's more than enough to go round. Me, Roy Burgess and Johnny Robinson each roll a raw potato into the embers to bake. We all love my mam's jacket spuds but nothing matches those cooked on the bonfire. After half an hour we use a stick to roll the spud out to see if they're cooked, but they're still hard.

Mr Ashworth takes on the job of setting off the fireworks. He carries a flash lamp and a glowing taper.

The firework display is magnificent, with colourful Roman Candles, Snow Fountains, Catherine Wheels, Sky Rockets, Bangers and Cannons. There's a couple of hairy moments though, when Mr Ashworth gingerly returns to a dud one, but as his face nears it, the thing returns to life and starts to pump out its coloured fireballs. Phew! That's a close one.

My mam then brings out the dishes of mushy peas and Mrs Priestly adds half a fresh Albert Hirst pie, to each portion.

We roll our burnt spuds out of the embers once again and let them cool. After ten minutes, Roy leads the way in peeling them: he strips the black, gritty skin off with his teeth to reveal the gorgeous, fluffy potato inside. We copy him. It's filthy, unhygienic but tastes divine.

Everyone's having a great time, especially when some of the teenagers secretly ignite a couple of Jumping Jacks just behind a group of revellers. Suddenly a scream is heard as the firework explodes then jumps, lands and explodes again. People roar with excitement but I'm not too keen. One Jumping Jack nearly goes down my welly and the other lands in Johnny Robinson's coat hood, only to jump out with a deafening bang.

Rob Rookledge

"Bleeding hell! Did you see that? It could have set my hair on fire!" says Johnny, as he checks the back of his head with his hand.

"Language!" shouts his dad. "There's ladies present!"

And I can't help thinking, how odd that using offensive language in front of a woman is treated more seriously than nearly having your head blown off.

Just at that moment, Mr Ashworth puts another rocket into a smoky milk bottle and lights it. As he retreats from the bottle, a big gust of wind blows it over and now it's pointing at the crowd. We all gasp in horror as the rocket fizzes for a nanosecond then whizzes just over our heads, zooms across the gardens and smashes into a house 100 yards away.

"Ey up! It's like playing war with real ammunition" says my mate Rob, as Kevin Robinson picks out a torn piece of tarpaulin from the fire with a stick. The tarpaulin is dripping molten tar and a couple of spots land on Rob's hand. He cries out and, as everyone turns to see what's happened but he has the presence of mind to dash to the bowl of water, which is used to defuse any unexploded fireworks. By plunging in his wounded hand, the pain immediately subsides, but Rob's still shaken up. Mrs Ashworth puts baby Adrian in his pushchair and fetches the family first aid kit. As she treats Rob with tender loving care, talking to him sympathetically and dabbing his brow, I feel a twinge of envy. Soon he returns to us, his mates, and I notice he's also developed a limp.

"You jammy swine" I say.

"Jammy? I might have lost my hand if it wasn't for Mrs Ashworth" he replies, and we both grin broadly.

Mr Rushforth, our head teacher at Agnes Road, warned us this morning about the dangers of fireworks but I doubt if anyone listened. I know I didn't. But as my mam often says: A good scare is better than good advice.

The display goes on for at least half an hour until we get to the biggest rocket, which is always left until last. It explodes with a reverberating boom, then crackles like giant pieces of brightly coloured Rice Crispies. The awe of the crowd is followed by a huge cheer and applause.

For the next two hours, fire engines can be heard emerging from the new Central Fire Station on Broadway and speeding on Keresforth Hall Road with sirens blaring. However, we hardly notice any of them because we're too busy enjoying ourselves. Mrs Gangley's hotdogs and onions soon disappear off the serving tray and Mr Copley, who hardly ever leaves the house, emerges with a tray full of his mother's homemade parkin.

By eight o'clock, a couple of big lads from Havelock Street, carefully lift up the sofa and gently place it on the flames. It's the final stick of fuel, and flames soon reach their highest. By now, people have had their fill of seasonal food and exciting pyrotechnical displays, so many have wondered off home to change out of their smoky clothes and watch TV.

Only teenagers are left, and for some, this is their first chance to chat-up someone they fancy. It's also a good opportunity to smoke a cigarette like their parents and spit in the fire to prove how 'big' they are.

Next morning our bonfire pile is just light, grey ash with a few wire springs on top.

I look in horror at our fence and coalhouse door. The green paint is all blistered. I forgot to drench it after I'd changed my clothes and Rob must have also got distracted. My mam says, not to worry, paint-blisters are a price worth paying for such a wonderful night and my dad will put it right.

In school assembly, Mr Rushforth lists the injuries to pupils the previous night but thank God there's been no deaths to report. Johnny Robinson whispers in my ear:

"That could have been me that Mr Rushforth's talking about" and just thinking about it makes me gulp like Alf Alfa.

Oh, we all adore Bonfire Night, even though, if we're honest, it scares us half to death.

TABLE TENNIS MANIA

It's Xmas Day 1964 and, among other gifts, my mam and dad buy me and my sister a basic table tennis set to share. It only contains one green net, two bats and four balls with a couple of metal fixtures to stretch the net and anchor it to a table. We don't even have a proper playing surface but like most families in the 1960s, we make-do with a wooden drop-leaf table, which meets our needs perfectly when opened out.

Straight after tea we all spend a couple of minutes moving the furniture to the sides to create a space for our new game.

"Look at the state of this shabby old suite" says my mam as she moves the sofa across the carpet with her knee. "It makes our house look like Steptoe's yard. I'm too embarrassed to invite guests, I am, honestly."

"There's nothing wrong with it at all, Mary" replies my dad trying to keep a straight face. "Look, it's still sturdy enough."

"Still sturdy enough? What about elegance and comfort?" says my mam. "And what about that awful tear on the arm? Why, this thing is nothing but a lump of garbage that's not fit for the bonfire, *and* it was third-hand; first your mother's, then your sister's and then ours."

"Alright, alright, I get the picture. You're not too impressed by it. Tell you what I'll do" says my dad chuckling because he knows he's been called out. "When one of these armchairs collapses I'll buy you a brand new suite. I can't say fairer than that, can I?" he adds, while tightening the table tennis net.

My mam's tone softens. "A brand new suite, did you say? Really? Are you serious? Whooo! That would be nice, Fred. I feel like I've won tonight's star prize on *Take Your Pick*" she says, laughing now. And I smile as I imagine her sabotaging one of the armchairs when no one's looking.

They're great entertainers, my mam and dad. Listening to them argue is funnier than listening to Hancock's Half Hour on the radio.

Oh, we do enjoy Christmas at our house because, although almost every room is freezing cold, we bank up the coal fire in the living room until it's roaring up the chimney back. Then we put down the draught excluders as insulation (including a woollen sock in the broken letter box) until we're nice and cosy, and finally we all join in a family game.

Nothing gives us greater pleasure than doing things together, and playing games in particular, is the source of endless joy and laughter.

The previous year we played Monopoly nearly every day for over a week and it got quite addictive. My dad finished up a millionaire every time and celebrated each day with a Tom Thumb (Christmas) cigar, like one of those property magnates you see on the BBC News; nevertheless, the rest of us still got a massive buzz from the thrills and spills of capitalist competition. However, by January 3rd, the trimmings were down, the tiny artificial tree was boxed-up and our Monopoly fun was soon forgotten.

This year it's sure to be similar, with one added treat: My mam's going to allow me and our Pauline to drink one small glass of alcohol. I ask for a Babycham with a cherry on a stick and my sister wants a Snowball. Cor, I'd love to be an adult. It must be great.

The table tennis games get off to a very clumsy start but it's not long before we all get the hang of it and exciting rallies become more regular.

Unfortunately, by late Boxing Day the competition has to be suspended because all four table-tennis balls have been accidentally crushed. Moreover, the next day's games are also postponed because "Sunday is a day of rest", says my dad, sanctimoniously. But we all know the real reason: Midwood Sports doesn't open until Monday at 10 am.

So, Monday morning at one minute to ten, I'm waiting with two shillings in my hand, outside the sports shop, as Bob Midwood himself unlocks the door.

"Ey up, Young 'Un! You're keen aren't you?" says Mr Midwood, using the first finger of each hand to smooth his fancy moustache.

"Yeah. I've got two bob, Mr Midwood, to buy four table tennis balls.

"Sorry, Son, we only sell them in boxes of six for half a crown" says Bob. You're a tanner short."

"What?" I look down at my two-bob piece feeling disconsolate, and Bob Midwood sees my terrible disappointment.

"I suppose I could split the box up and sell the balls separately? Hmmm. But no I shouldn't really. Tell you what I'll do. Seeing as it's Christmas I'll let you have the whole box for two shillings" says Bob.

"What? Really?" I can't believe it and I feel like doing one of those flamboyant Irish jigs like Ebenezer Scrooge does in that wonderful Christmas film.

Later that evening the furniture's moved once again, the fire's banked up and the draught excluders are in place. Now it's time for serious table tennis, and we're all dead excited.

My dad does a proper draw like they do on the radio for the FA Cup, but he puts everyone's name into his flat cap. The fixtures are then written on a card and stuck to the kitchen door, so that it covers up the unsightly pin-pricks caused by those who couldn't hit the dart board.

The games are always close which means everyone's interest is maintained, and the volume on the TV is turned down completely to avoid distractions.

My mam is so funny and always up for a laugh. If she's beaten by my dad's quick serve she always says (whilst holding a cigarette in her left hand)

"Hold your horses. You can just go and take that serve again, Fred. I wasn't ready, was I kids?"

But when she's serving to him she'll deliver it when he's not looking and insist it counts.

"Tut! Is that a cobweb up there on the ceiling" she'll say, staring upwards, then quick as a flash, her serve will bounce across the table like a pond-skimmer, to win the point. However, she's different when she plays me and our Pauline - she usually lets us win.

Soon my Dad also invents this clever forfeit: The person who comes last in any one session has to make a cup of tea for the rest of us. Consequently, we're all desperate to avoid last place because there's no heating in our kitchen (We call it Siberia) except when the gas cooker's on. Brrrrr!

On Wednesday evening I perform badly but it's no big deal because even if I come last today, I'll still be top of the table tennis league. However, I will have to honour the forfeit and make the tea.

Mam needs only one point to beat Dad but then there's major controversy. My dad hits the ball and it just grazes the edge of the table at my mam's side, meaning he's stolen the point.

Strictly speaking, that makes me favourite to do the honours but my mam's having none of it.

"Oh, bad luck, Fred" she says, doffing her cigarette in the ashtray and walking away from the table with a superior look on her face. Our Pauline splutters with laughter.

"What? It clipped the edge of the table, Mary. It's my point" complains Dad.

"Oh no it's not" she says as though she's at the pantomime. "Anyway, I'm off to Siberia now to make a pot of tea. Our Ronnie will tell you that it was miles off the table, won't you, love?"

I take a long deep breath and let the air hiss out of my swollen cheeks and pursed lips.

"Nope. I'm sorry, Dad. I didn't see or hear a thing" I say, shaking my head and crossing my fingers behind my back. Then I sit down to await the cuppa that I should have made.

Me and my sister are always on my mam's side in a dispute and my dad pretends he minds but he doesn't really. In fact, he quite enjoys sending himself up.

I envy my dad because he's able to laugh even in defeat. I wish I could. I'm more likely to make a fool of myself by throwing a wobbly. Obviously, I wouldn't dream of throwing a punch at anyone in my family but to be frank, seeing me in defeat is not a sight I'm proud of.

By Sunday 3rd January our table tennis mania has reached its climax. Dad says he's got a special dispensation from the vicar of St Edward's to hold the final evening of the tournament tonight, even though it's the Sabbath. Besides, he's back at work on 'nights' tomorrow.

He also announces that the winner of the championship will receive this wonderful silver cup on a plinth that he lifts down from the bureau. Dad niftily turns the plinth round to hide the inscription, which reads,

"To The World's Greatest Bingo Player"

We all think it's funny but I'm really looking forward to being presented with it. All I have to do is beat Father today and it's mine.

Tonight everything is taken more seriously so there's no mucking about. I can't believe the speed and length of the rallies. I play my dad in the final game and the winner of the whole thing hinges on this one match. It's 21 – 20 to my Dad and he's serving to win but he presents me with a simple shot to draw level and I smash it! Unfortunately, I miss the table completely, so the point and the championship belongs to him.

Absolute silence ensues.

No one moves, not even a twitch.

We all wonder what could possibly happen next.

Inside I'm a raging torrent and my mam, dad and sister know me too well to taunt me.

If *I'd* hit the winning point I'd be jumping up and down celebrating, but I haven't and I'm not.

I try to keep calm. If I can control myself for half a minute I'll be okay.

I can walk away from the table with dignity.

Come on Ronnie Steele, I say to myself, you can do it. After all, only mourngy babies throw tantrums. You've got no excuses. Dignity, dignity, dignity.

"You took that serve before I was ready!" I shout at my dad, and I can see he's doing his best to display a mournful expression, not a triumphant one.

I look at my mam. She looks away quickly and is also trying hard to appear sad by turning down the corners of her mouth.

Our Pauline is sat on the chair arm with both hands up to her face. Is she trying to subdue a laugh an' all?

Dad can't hold on to his pretend melancholy any longer and his face is twisting into a smile. His shoulders start to move up and down as if he's laughing silently, then at last he makes a kind of sneezing noise.

"What's so funny?" I demand loudly.

"Nothing, nothing" says my Dad, roaring by now. "I've just remembered... a joke I heard... um... yesterday." And he's actually laughing so much now, he can't even talk.

"What joke?" I ask, getting madder and madder." Come on, what joke?"

"I can't remember now" says my Dad but it was so funny. Best one I've ever heard."

Now my Mam and sister are struggling to hold back the laughter. Our Pauline's drops her hands from her face, throws her head back, is screaming with mirth, and tears are streaming down her cheeks; while my mam tries her very best to pretend she's actually sobbing, not laughing, just to spare my feelings.

That's it. I've had enough. I can't stand anymore. So I smash the ping-pong ball so hard against the wall it rebounds off the chair arm and finishes up on the coal fire and bursts into flames like a hissing solar flare. This just makes things worse and I see all three of my family lying on the carpet or armchair, holding their sides because they hurt too much from laughing.

Then my little rubber-coated bat also finishes up flying out of my hand and hitting the dividing wall between us and the Ashworth's.

Typical Ronnie Steele - when will I grow up?

MAM AND HER NEW SUITE

The day after the table-tennis final, we're all sitting in the living room eating corned beef hash and pancakes. My Dad is in *his* armchair nearest the TV, when suddenly the springs under his seat give way and his backside finishes up on the carpet.

"Look at that!" he says. "Not a morsel spilt." And it's true, the Daily Mirror's under his plate and he's holding it level. However, he's stuck in the chair and it takes all three of us to rescue his dinner and pull him clear.

After lunch, my sister and I go out to play with friends. Mam, remembering Dad's promise about a new suite, goes next door to tell Mrs Priestley the good news.

When all three of us return to the house, we find Dad's been busy. We know he's brilliant at many things but DIY is NOT one of them.

"Look at this armchair, Mary. It's like new" says he. And I must admit, from where I'm standing, the busted chair does look remarkably like it did before the springs fell out. My Mam goes to explore further, by lifting up the seat-cushion to inspect underneath. Yep, all the springs have definitely disappeared and in their place is an ill-fitting piece of old plywood. Mam lifts up the plywood and says,

"What are you talking about... 'it looks like new'? It looks more like a bloody wig on a bald man's head!"

Now it's me and our Pauline that's falling about laughing, but my dad's not even listening.

"I just needed four small pieces of wood to nail across the four corners of the seat frame" he says. "So, I sawed up the table-tennis bats and nailed 'em to the corners. Then I discovered this large piece of plywood in the shed. It fits on top of the bats perfectly. Just try sitting on it, Mary. Go on. You'll be amazed."

My Mam plonks down in the chair with a judder. It's feels like sitting down on a solid stone wall.

"It'll put us on until we can afford a new suite" says my dad, proudly admiring his Flintstone-style handiwork.

I sense Mam is about to explode.

"Put us on? Put us on!?! You can neddy" says Mam. "You might be on the night-shift tonight but tomorrow it's Wigfalls for us two. I'm getting a brand new suite like you promised.

"Okay" replies my dad. "If you really think it's necessary."

By the time my dad sets off on his push-bike for Dodworth Colliery, the trimmings are down, the artificial tree is boxed-up and our ping pong mania is just a pleasant memory.

Another wonderful family Christmas is over and our appetite for table tennis is exhausted, which is just as well really.

HARRY COPS A BLINDER

It's late afternoon in June, 1965, and the hot sun is beaming down on our junior school cricket match against St Mary's. We play all our home games on Shawland's Field – formerly known as the Preston-Robert's Field, which is a huge, sloping area that contains one football pitch but is big enough to contain four. Right in the middle of the field is a cricket strip made of bitumen that is two yards wide and about 25 yards long. At the bottom of the field are two brick-built air-raid shelters and to the side nearest Holgate Grammar School is an underground shelter that's been filled in.

"Two, four, six and a quarter,

Who are we going to slaughter?

St Fairies!" shout half a dozen Agnes Road youngsters.

Today is a cup-tie and the gorgeous weather has drawn quite a large crowd of noisy supporters for both teams. We sit near the top of the field with our backs to the proper Shaw Lane ground where Barnsley Cricket Club and Yorkshire County Cricket Club, sometimes play.

Both teams are very well turned out. Every player wears a white t-shirt, shorts, socks and plimsolls.

Our cricket pads are a dazzling white, and as I stare at them I begin to recall the lousy weekend I've just had because of them.

It was immediately after last Friday's game against St Helen's that Mr Bates asked if anyone could take the pads home and whiten them?

"Yes, I can do that, Mr Bates" I said, remembering my sister has a tube of whitening that she uses for her own school plimsolls. But when I get home and tell my mam, she goes bonkers.

"Eight pads to whiten. Eight bloody pads? And where are we going to get the whitening for eight pads? And who's going to pay for it?

I'd learnt it's best not to argue the toss with my mam when she's being unreasonable.

After using all our Pauline's whitening I only managed to treat one half of a single pad, so I go into town and buy a bottle of whitening from Woolies. When I return home I've only half a crown change from a ten bob note, and that means I'll have to do a lot of errands to pay Mam back.

The whitening job isn't easy. It takes me and Rob Rookledge, most of Saturday afternoon and all Sunday morning in our back garden, smartening up all eight pads.

Then my mother starts on about it again: "And I bet *you* didn't volunteer to whiten the pads, did you Robert? No, of course not because you've more oil in your lamp, haven't you?" says she, not even waiting for an answer.

I catch Rob nodding and shaking his head, and even tutting. The rotten traitor.

"You're a creep" I whisper in his ear.

"Nay, I wasn't the one who offered to whiten the pads for Mr Bates" he whispers back, smirking.

Whooo, sometimes I feel like punching Robert, I really do, but at least he's helped me to whiten the pads, I suppose.

Ian Bailey's voice wakes me up from yet another daydream and I'm back in the here and now.

"Fifty runs should be enough to see us through to the semi" he says as he unbuckles his pad and throws off his batting gloves.

"Bad luck, Ian. It was a right catch that got you out, mate, but you should be pleased with a knock of fifteen" I tell him, without taking my eyes off the play.

Some of our noisy, younger supporters have lost interest in the game and are gathering the newly-cut grass into small heaps and throwing it at each other. Oh, I love the smell of cut grass.

Then suddenly, I feel a pile of grass being dumped on my head and when I look round I see Norman Lofthouse laughing and running away. Norman is not his real name. He's been given this nickname because he's a Norman-know-it-all who reckons he's an expert on everything under the sun. He gets on my nerves.

"Not picked for the team again, Norman" I say, teasing. "Bit o' bad luck you're having.

"Batesie did ask me to be stumper today but I said I wasn't much bothered" says Norman, telling lies again. "In fact, my old head teacher at Ward Green, Mr Lodge, reckons, one day, I might be wicket keeper for England."

This causes all of us to laugh out loud.

"Aye, I bet he does" says Rob Rookledge who then proceeds to shout at the top of his voice, like a newspaper vendor: "Norman's Weekly Liar! Come and get your copy of Norman's weekly liar! On sale here! Only sixpence!"

Then, a massive cheer erupts from the St Mary's fans that pulls our attention back to the game. Paul Merryweather is run out after a smart piece of fielding.

"47 should still do it" says Rob Rookledge as he helps Harry Stott, our regular wicketkeeper, to get padded up.

Meanwhile, as the St Mary's boys get ready to bat, our players position themselves in the field. We're all very confident because we have our secret weapon, Arnie Sidebottom, who bats brilliantly, bowls incredibly fast and has played in the school team since he was only eight.

There are only three fielding positions that are really important: the wicketkeeper - and we have the best in Harry Stott; the long-stop - and we have Rob Rookledge, who has a great throwing arm; and the bowlers - Arnie and Paul Merryweather, who are both outstanding.

Arnie Sidebottom starts the bowling and knocks the stumps over twice in the first over without St Mary's scoring, so it's obviously going to be a walk-over.

Harry Stott

Those little kids from our school set up another chant:

"Easy! Easy! Easy!"

I think to myself, what a fearsome sight Arnie Sidebottom is to any batsman. He's got short ginger hair, loads of freckles and can whip the ball down the wicket. Another feature which is perhaps less endearing is his untidiness.

"Oi, Arnold! Get your shirt tucked in and pull your socks up" bawls his dad as he watches from the boundary. Arnie's shirt is quickly tucked in and his white socks are raised to the knee but two minutes later he's back to his normal, untidy self. Personally, I quite like his untidiness because it makes him unique – a bit like Georgie Best with his long hair. I've a good mind to roll down my socks and wear my shirt outside my shorts, too.

There are no more incidents for a while but then comes a sickener that alters the game completely. Harry Stott, our wicketkeeper, has to stand well back from the spring-loaded stumps because Arnie's deliveries sometimes thud head-high into his padded gloves. All it takes is one miscalculation on Harry's part and there could be real problems and soon my anxieties come to pass. One of Arnie's deliveries bounces high over the stumps and flies towards Harry face. Harry thinks he's got it covered but instead he gets caught with a blinder, right in the middle of his forehead.

There's a big groan from the crowd and screams from some mothers because they can see immediately that it's a serious blow.

Harry's lying down on the bitumen surface moaning as everyone races to help. By the time I get there, a massive egg-shaped swelling has appeared on his forehead. No one seems to know what to do but by sheer chance a hospital consultant comes to the rescue.

Arnie Sidebottom

Mr Nkombua is currently living in digs at the Sidebottom's house on Clarendon Street while he's working at St Helen's Hospital at Gawber. He's been watching the game from the boundary with Arnie's father. He runs over to administer first aid, and everyone's ordered to move back to give him more room.

"You'll be all right, liddle boy" he says, looking at the growing lump. "Can you tell me what happened?"

"What happened? We all saw what happened" says Norman-Know-It-All

"Yeah" says Ian "but he might be trying to calm Harry down and find out if he's concussed."

"Oh, yeah, that's what I was thinking" says Norman, lying again.

That's what I like about Ian Bailey, he's smart.

Harry's still sobbing but he's alert enough to answer the doctor's question.

"Will someone fetch me an ice lolly?" says the doctor as he now turns back to the injured hero to ask him how many fingers he's holding up.

Meanwhile, Rob Rookledge speeds off down to Derek Sharland's corner shop on Shaw Street to beg an ice lolly for the doctor.

"Funny time to crave an ice lolly" says Norman, but as the doctor rips off the wrapper and applies the lolly to Harry's bump, Norman says, "Yeah, of course, the ice lolly is for the swelling, obviously. Anyone knows that."

"What's tha know about first aid?" I say to Norman.

"Only what my Grandad tells me. He's used to be chief surgeon at Becketts" replies Norman.

The badly wounded soldier is helped off the bitumen pitch and taken to sit down with the scorers where Mr Nkombua can monitor him.

"Norman says he's a good stumper, Mr Bates. Can he replace Harry?" I helpfully suggest.

"Really? Are you a wicketkeeper, Norman?" asks our teacher.

It sounds comical hearing Mr Bates using Norman's nickname. It's because Norman's new to our school and Mr Bates has no idea what his real name is.

Norman doesn't know what to say. I don't think he fancies trying to catch a howitzer from Arnie.

"Erm... I'd love to help you out, Mr Bates, but I've got this stiff shoulder, you see" answers Norman, circling his right arm like a wheel and cringing with pain.

"No problem" says Mr Bates, "we'll manage.

Consequently, Paul Merryweather is sacrificed as a bowler and becomes the new wicketkeeper. Mr Bates then chooses me as the stand-in bowler but I make a hash of it.

"Don't try and bowl too fast, Ronnie Steele" says Mr Bates "and pitch the ball up to the batter." I do neither and am replaced at the end of my only over, feeling disappointed.

Two other bowlers are tried but neither of them are much cop. The incident with Harry, also seems to have upset Arnie because he's decided not to bowl with as much pace. As a consequence the two St Mary's batsmen are starting to build up their confidence and their score.

Steve 'Bonner' Brown is their captain and a bit special as a sportsman. At the other end is nippy Paul Wilkinson who keeps playing the ball off his legs and down the slope to where the goals posts are on the football field. They once score four runs off Paul's shot before Rob manages to reach Paul Merryweather with his long throw.

The St Mary's players and supporters are smiling now and are well on their way to victory, so Harry Stott declares himself fit again to return to the game. God he's brave! Unfortunately for him, Mr Nkombua has other ideas and firmly refuses to allow him back on the pitch.

With only thirteen runs needed to win, St Mary's have to face another competent bowler, John Ripley, and it's at this juncture that Arnie Sidebottom decides to bowl his fastest once again.

Suddenly, the two best St Mary's batsmen are back with their team mates as wickets begin to tumble. When John Ripley gets their last man caught at long stop, St Mary's are still five short of our total.

We're delighted with the victory but all we can think of at this moment is Harry Stott. So we all dash over to see how he is and he's not a pretty sight. As he tries to smile, Harry shows his two chipped front teeth. We're used to seeing them but the doctor isn't.

"Hey, I didn't know you'd broken your teeth as well" he says, thinking the bump on the head and the broken teeth are connected.

Harry laughs in a half-hearted way and tells the doctor his teeth have been chipped for years.

Meanwhile, our captain, Arnie, is shouting at the top of his voice, "Three cheers for... um... um... St Mary's! Hip! Hip..."

But no one finishes it off with an "hurray" because the moment's gone.

When we realise that Harry's okay, we start to put the bats, gloves and pads back into the long leather bag and we notice there are two or three dark scuff marks on my beautiful pads.

"Do you fancy taking them home Ronnie and whitening them again?" says Rob Rookledge, trying not to smile.

"No I don't Robert but I'll tell you what I do fancy - I fancy taking one of these cricket bats and playing wacko with it."

And on the word 'wacko' I pick up a bat and chase after him, making the sound of a crazed monster but he's away on his toes. However, Norman-Know-It-All is not so alert, so I manage to wallop him with a couple of cow-tailers on the backside before he's able to dodge out of reach.

AFTERWORD

Less than eight years later, Arnie Sidebottom is making his debut for Manchester United FC against Chelsea at Stamford Bridge. He's also making great progress in achieving his other great ambition; that is, to represent his county and his country at his first love, cricket.

MR GLOVER, SUPER-HERO (1970)

(Wes Hobson, former Barnsley Chronicle photographer, now freelance, reminisces about his former school teacher, Brian Glover.)

You don't mess about in Mr Glover's class. No one does, and I must admit, at first he scares me half to death. However, I now realise that as long as you do your work and behave yourself, he's as right as rain.

Mr Glover teaches English and Games at Racecommon Road Secondary Modern School. If we play football or cricket, he usually takes part in the game himself and plays to win. It's obvious that he loves sport, takes it seriously and always sticks firmly to the rules – even if it means defeat.

I remember, very clearly, one cricketing incident last summer:

We're on the school playground nearest Racecommon Road and Mr Glover is captain of England who are fielding. He's bowling and I'm batting for Australia but I'm standing at the bowler's end, ready to run. I hear Mr Glover taking a short run-up as I start to walk towards the batter's end. But instead of letting go of the ball, Mr Glover whips off my bails, and because my bat is an inch outside my crease, I'm run-out. But anyone who knows anything about cricket is aware that this tactic is the worst kind of gamesmanship.

Good sportsmen should always give the batter a warning.

 "You're out, Wesley!" bellows the England medium-pace bowler and umpire, as he picks up the bails.

"What?" I shout back in dismay. "You can't do that, Mr Glover! That's not fair play!"

"If the umpire raises his first finger, Wesley, then you're back in the pavilion, lad. No argument" says Mr Glover as he stands resolutely with his finger still in the air.

"But you're playing for England. How can you umpire fairly if you're playing for one of the teams on the pitch?" I argue.

"Life is unfair Wesley, so get used to it. It's your responsibility to ensure you never give your opponents a chance to prosper from your good nature, lad. I suggest if you have a complaint then you put it in writing and send it to the head of PE" he adds, with a grin.

"But *you're* the acting head of PE? I say, and I suddenly find it impossible to keep a straight face at the ridiculous no-win situation I find myself in.

I have to 'walk' and England then have the edge.

From that day onwards I learn that Mr Glover remains a stickler for observing the rules, even if it means penalising his own team. In this respect he's very different to his portrayal of Mr Sugden in the film, *Kes*. In real life he's the champion of both fairness and the underdog, and certainly NOT an inveterate bully.

Furthermore, after this salutary lesson on the cricket pitch I'm always careful never to get run-out at the bowler's end. And despite my exasperation at his intransigence as an umpire, I'm growing to love this guy - and I'm not the only one who feels this way. When I talk to the other lads and lasses in my class they all say the same:

"Aye he's all right, is Glover" and I know that means a heck of a lot when it comes out of the mouths of stroppy adolescents.

I particularly like the way he addresses me as Wesley. Some teachers use only our surnames, others don't bother learning our names at all, but Mr Glover calls me Wesley.

I let my mam know.

"Mr Glover always calls me Wesley, Mam" I tell her one hot summer's evening while she's trying to watch Coronation Street.

"Well, what's wrong with that, Wes? That's your name isn't it?" she says as she takes her eyes off the screen. What's up? Don't you like your name?"

"Yeah" I answer "but nobody on earth calls me Wesley."

"Well, I can't see your problem then."

"Hmmm, I suppose you're right, Mam. There's nothing wrong with my full Christian name. And yeah, I actually quite like him calling me Wesley when I think about it."

I'm very small for my age and perhaps because of this I find I can get away with things that others can't. Gradually I learn that Mr Glover doesn't mind when I make a witty quip (as long as it's not designed to make him look a fool) because I see him smiling. This is highly unusual at Racecommon Road Secondary Modern School. Perhaps other teachers would find my attempts at humour subversive but I doubt that Mr Glover would ever feel his control is under threat from his students.

I just wish I could make the school football team. I love the game but because I'm the smallest in my year I'm always picked as sub. I'm fast, strong and competitive – a bit like a young Billy Bremner, I like to think – but Mr Glover always gives me the subs shirt. It gets me down a bit and so I fantasise sometimes about having supernatural powers. I used to love watching Batman and Robin and always imagined myself as Bruce Wayne's assistant. If only...

Today our school football team is playing away at Royston Secondary Modern. There are some tough kids there.

It's the first half, the sun is shining and we're playing uphill in our all-white Leeds United strip. I'm the sub again of course and Mr Glover and I are standing just off the pitch on the halfway line. Directly opposite us are a bunch of 11 to 15 year old Royston fans. Things aren't going too well for us. Royston have a midfielder called Paul Brooks, who's an exceptional player, and he's causing us all sorts of problems. Sometimes he dribbles straight past our best defenders as though they're not there.

The Royston supporters are looking in our direction and chanting something but it's hard to make out exactly what it is. It sounds like Ashford or Dashford or something. However, as all half-dozen of them join in the chanting together, their words float across to us more clearly. They seem to be looking and pointing at us and I can just make out some of the words:

"Who's Cat Dashford? Who's Cat Dashford? Who's Cat Dashford?"

"Ah, it's nice to see young lads enjoying themselves" Mr Glover says to me, smiling.

However, by then I've managed to decipher that the lads are having a laugh at Mr Glover's expense because they're not shouting "Who's","Cat" or "Dashford".

"Erm... I think they're shouting something insulting, Mr Glover" I reply.

"What?"

"It's definitely an insult, Mr Glover."

"An insult?" says he, as their chanting reaches a crescendo.

"You fat bastard! You fat bastard! You fat bastard!"

I feel really upset and angry for Mr Glover.

Some of our players have lost concentration. They've stopped chasing the football and instead are moving towards the noisy Royston fans. But before open warfare breaks out, I hear Mr Glover shouting at the top of his voice:

"Racecommon Road! Focus on the game! Play to the whistle! John Turner, get back in that goal, now!"

I wonder what Mr Glover's going to do?

Then he starts talking to me out of the corner of his mouth while appearing to follow the game.

"Wesley, who would you pick out as the ringleader from that bunch of reprobates over yonder?"

"That tall lad wearing the red jumper" I reply.

"Hmmm... me too. Follow me, Wesley" replies Mr Glover, as he sets off walking round the football pitch.

I'm nervous and excited. How on earth will he sort them out? He's one of the few teachers who never hits kids.

As we pass behind our goal at the bottom of the slope I notice the trouble-makers have stopped chanting and are starting to look uncomfortable.

"We'll sort 'em for you at half time, Sir" says our keeper but Mr Glover's not listening. By the time we reach the corner flag I notice some of the trouble-makers have started to hop from one foot to the other but no one's scared enough to make a run for it.

Meanwhile, John Turner is stood on the edge of his penalty area, pointing at the small lad in the Royston group.

"Cocky get!" bellows John.

When Mr Glover reaches the group he brushes the small lad aside like a pesky insect and grabs the tall one by the throat. Putting his face really close up to him he bawls:

"Shut-your-face!" then lets go.

The tall one has been put in his place, but the little cheeky one mumbles quietly:

"Fat bastard."

Suddenly, Mr Glover reaches over to grab his hand and raises it above his head. However, he's is not actually holding the kid's hand - he's grabbed only his little finger. It must be a wrestling or karate hold or something. It doesn't hurt the kid except when he tries to wriggle free, so, to avoid discomfort the cheeky one has to freeze like a statue. After about 10 seconds, Mr Glover has proved his point and lets go.

"Come on Wesley. Our business here is finished" says Mr Glover and we walk briskly away.

The tormenting chants come to a sudden stop.

As we pass behind our goal, on our return to our position on the touchline, I'm feeling on top of the world. I imagine that Mr Glover is Batman and I'm his trusted assistant, Robin. We didn't half show them who was boss, and I find myself punching my right fist into the palm of my left hand, saying "Holy gang of thugs!" under my breath, as I smile unconsciously.

"What the devil are you smiling at?" asks Mr Glover.

I clear my throat and quick as a flash retort,

"Why did the school teacher go for an eye-sight test?"

"I don't know" answers Mr Glover. "Why did the school teacher go for an eye-sight test?"

"Cos he couldn't control his pupils."

Mr Glover gives a hearty laugh and says,

"Hmmm. Not bad that, Wesley. Might use that in the staffroom on Monday" he replies. "I'm sure Mr Kaye will like it."

At half-time Mr Glover focuses on making sure we contain Royston's star player, Paul Brooks.

"You guys must take no prisoners" says Mr Glover. "I want to see 11 Skinner Normantons out there in the second half. You play with passion when you wear the colours of our proud school!"

All the players nod their heads but I'm fairly certain none of us are 100% sure what he means by "take no prisoners".

"Ey up" whispers Alan Earp, who's taken an evening off delivering newspapers to play for the school team today. "Who the hell's Skinner Normanton?"

"The Norman Hunter of his day" I whisper back.

Mr Glover turns to Geoff Smith, our skipper, and says, "I don't want to see any dirty play but I want to draw your attention to the 11th Commandment."

Geoff Smith looks puzzled.

"11th Commandment?" repeats Geoff, screwing his face up, like you do when someone's talking nonsense. "Thought there were only 10 Commandments."

Mr Glover says, "The 11th Commandment is for defenders only, Geoffrey, and it states:

'Thou shalt not pass!' Gerrit?"

As the penny drops, Geoff smiles. He's got the message, all right. Brooksy will never dribble past him again.

It's time for the second half and as Mr Glover and I return to our place I suggest another solution to the problem of Paul Brooks.

"Do you want me to get out my air-gun, Mr Glover, and deal with Paul Brooks?" I say, tongue in cheek.

"Don't be stupid, Wesley. That would be a waste of a good pellet" he replies, smiling and ruffling my hair.

Eventually, Batman does give his partner a brief run-out on the right wing and his half-time pep talk definitely makes our team harder to dribble past. But unfortunately, my inclusion as super-sub doesn't affect the final result. We're beaten.

Nevertheless, I'll not forget this day. It's the nearest I've ever come to feeling like a super-hero, thanks to The Caped Crusader himself, Brian Glover.

What an extraordinary guy. We all loved him.

1969... BRIAN GLOVER – A HEART IN A HEARTLESS WORLD

Diane Royston is a 15 year old student at Racecommon Road Secondary Modern School. She lives up Worsbrough Common with her mam, dad and 13 year old brother, Dan.

Diane's father is a very sickly man. He's suffers from a serious heart condition which first became apparent in 1958 when, whilst suffering a heart attack, he was stretchered from the coal face at Woolley Colliery. He's all skin and bone, weighing a little over five stones.

Her dad's illness casts the family into serious poverty. Mrs Royston can't work because her husband needs 24 hour care. Although they get assistance with their council house rent and the children get free school meals, surviving is a continual struggle. They have to scrimp and scrape and there's nothing left at the end of the week to spend on leisure. However, they're a very proud family, who create a fine clean home by disciplined austerity.

Diane is a bright and bonny 15 year old. She's a bit of a rebel who is prepared to fiercely defend her family, especially her little brother, if necessary. She's not that fond of school but adores her English teacher, Mr Glover. He sees real promise in her – she's polite, hardworking, an inveterate reader and an accomplished story writer. So, when Mr Glover needs volunteers to play parts in Animal Farm, Diane is chosen to play Napoleon.

She takes to her role like a duck to water and the play turns into a great success.

She's also good at Maths but likes to send herself up by pretending to use her fingers when calculating simple arithmetic. Moreover, Diane has a decent voice and if you listen to her singing a Cilla Black song you'd swear it was Cilla herself who was singing.

One day, during an English lesson, it's discovered that a small amount of change has gone missing from Lynn Manterfield's bag in the cloakroom and

Mr Glover has to sort it out. He instructs everybody to bring their coats and bags into the classroom.

"This is most unpleasant" says Mr Glover. "If anyone wants to admit their guilt and they let me know now or at break time, then a written apology will suffice and I'll take the matter no further."

The class is silent.

"Ok, then. Empty all your pockets and bags and put everything on the desk in front of you."

The students are not too happy about this but Mr Glover has their respect and so his orders are carried out. Then he walks round the room shaking coats and bags to listen for the jingle-jangle of coins.

"Mr Glover" says Alan Earp. I've got a bag full of coppers in my bag for the shop after school. I brought it from home."

This is followed by a plethora of complaints:

"I've got some change too and I've not nicked it."

"Just because we have money doesn't mean we've stolen it."

"I've got some coins from my dinner money in..."

Mr Glover realises he's made an error of judgement.

"Okay, okay, okay" he shouts. "Calm down, nobody is accusing anyone of anything – yet."

But Mr Glover's mind is now focussed on something completely different. He's noticed something very odd about the contents of Diane's bag.

"Put all your belongings away and we'll try and sort it later. Oh and Diane, I'd like to see you on the playground at break-time to discuss the Animal Farm play" says Mr Glover as he collects up the text books.

On the playground Mr Glover sips his coffee as Diane approaches him with her friend, Lynn.

"Would you do me a favour, Lynn? Fetch me a bag of Jelly Babies from the Top Shop, will you? I'll share them out last lesson."

Mr Glover loves sweets.

As Lynn disappears through the wrought iron gates and onto Racecommon Road, Mr Glover pours away a drop of coffee that's spilled into his saucer.

"Now then, Diane. I've sent Lynn to the shop so I can speak to you alone."

Diane's all ears.

"I've noticed you don't stay for school dinners, do you?"

"No Sir."

"It's all right, Diane, you can call me Mr Glover - I've not been knighted yet.

"Yes Sir... I mean, yes, Mr Glover."

"Do you go home for your dinner then?"

"No, I bring a packed lunch."

"Hmmm, that's interesting because when you emptied your duffle bag in the classroom I noticed it didn't contain a packed lunch and your form teacher says you and your brother qualify for free school meals."

Diane's expression alters immediately and she looks away as tears begin to well up. Mr Glover gets out a large white handkerchief and says,

"Oh dear. I didn't mean to upset you. Here you are Diane. Go back into school and get yourself tidied up. If any teachers or prefects try to stop you, tell them to come and see me. Will you come to my classroom at about 12:30 and we'll discuss this further?"

"I'm not in trouble am I, Mr Glover" asks Diane, as she dabs her eyes while other girls look on curiously.

"No, no, no. Not at all but I'd like to get to the bottom of this."

At 12:30 sharp, Diane climbs the stone steps and enters the old boys' block where Mr Glover has his classroom.

"And where the devil do you think you're going?" asks Miss Wraith, her form teacher. Miss Wraith, who also teaches Physics, has a permanent scowl on her face as though she's just had a spoonful of nasty medicine.

"I've to go and see Mr Glover. He's asked me to..."

"Oh no you're not" interrupts Miss Wraith. "Mr Glover's busy and you know the rules: Only staff and prefects may re-enter school at lunchtime."

"But..."

"No buts about it. You're not coming in. And by the way, what's that on your face? Don't tell me you're wearing make-up?" She then wets her finger and draws it down Diane's cheek in order to prove her point.

Miss Wraith studies her finger. "Hmmm... as I thought... make-up!"

"No it isn't!" shouts Diane as she uses her sleeve to wipe the wetness off her cheek. I never wear make-up for school but I can see *you've* got some caked on."

"How dare you! How dare you speak to me like that!" replies the furious Miss Wraith. "You impudent girl! Go to Mr Kaye's office immediately! And if I see you in school wearing shoes with heels like that again, you'll be sent straight home!"

Diane doesn't say anything more but the expression on her face displays utter contempt. Her eyes move slowly from Miss Wraith's face, down to the stiletto-heeled shoes she's wearing. It's obvious to Miss Wraith what she's thinking.

As Diane goes to wait outside of the headteacher's office for her punishment, Mr Glover notices she's late and so despatches prefects to find her. He's very concerned because Diane's not one to miss an appointment.

With five minutes to go before the end of the lunch hour, she finally enters Mr Glover's form room.

"I've heard you've been in trouble with Miss Wraith, Diane" says Mr Glover.

"Yes. She wouldn't allow me into school" she replies, looking down at her shoes. What Diane really wants to say is, "Miss Wraith is a bitch" but she thinks better of it. Instead she says, "At the start of this school year she got on to me so much, my mam had to come up to complain about her to Mr Kaye. She's really got it in for me, Mr Glover."

"Hmmm, Miss Wraith didn't mention that when I bumped into her 10 minutes ago. But I've no time to discuss that now. I just want to know why you had no packed lunch in your bag this morning."

"I gave it to my brother, Dan, to look after."

"Diane. I want you to tell me the whole truth. I can't help you unless you do. You see I've already spoken to your friend, Lynn, who tells me you qualify for free school meals but you refuse them and go hungry at..."

Suddenly the bell for the end of lunchtime blasts out.

"Oh bother!" says Mr Glover. Come and see me at four o'clock and we'll sort it then" he says, as he takes out a large green booklet from his drawer for afternoon registration.

"I'm sorry Mr Glover but I can't. Every Wednesday evening I work down at the fruit market in town."

"Well, what about seeing me in the morning at 8:30 before school begins?" he asks.

"Sorry, Mr Glover but I deliver the daily papers every morning and don't arrive at school until quarter to nine."

"Ok then, we'll meet in my room tomorrow lunchtime. And bring your friend. Oh and don't you worry about Miss Wraith. I'll smooth things over with her" he says, as his registration class line up noisily in the hall, just outside his room.

Mr Glover is full of charm. No wonder everyone loves him.

When Diane enters her own form room, Miss Wraith has a face like thunder which she maintains for the rest of the afternoon.

*   *   *   *   *   *   *   *

It's Thursday lunchtime and as Miss Wraith walks through the hall she sees Mr Glover in his form room talking animatedly to Diane and Lynn Manterfield. She'd love to know what they're talking about. Why doesn't Brian ever choose to have a cosy chat with me, she thinks?

She taps on his classroom door, lifts the brass latch and with a radiant smile says,

"I'm just making a coffee, Mr Glover. Would you like me to bring you one?"

"That's very kind of you, Miss Wraith. Yes please and could you bring two more for these two lovely girls?"

Miss Wraith's face suddenly changes and she bangs the door shut in a tantrum.

Then Mr Glover says:

"Okay, Diane. Let me get this straight. You qualify for free school meals but you prefer packed lunches. However, you never bring a packed lunch to school. That means you're going from breakfast until tea without any nourishment. Why? I just don't understand."

Diane's eyes begin to fill up again, so her friend, Lynn, speaks up for her.

"I can explain, Mr Glover. Her mam and dad think she has a free school meal every day but she's not had anything to eat at lunchtime for nearly two years. She daren't tell them because they'll go mad. It all started when Mr Sheridan was our form teacher. He made us form two lines for the dinner register - one for those who pay and one for those who get them free, and now Miss Wraith does the same. It's so embarrassing for those who can't pay. They're treated like scum, Mr Glover. Not all form teachers do it that way. I just think some do it to humiliate the poor kids."

There's silence for a few seconds as Mr Glover leans back in his chair and considers what Lynn has just told him.

"Your parents should know about this, Diane" he says.

"Oh no!" says Diane, loudly. "Please don't tell them. They'll be very hurt if you do."

"And what about your brother? Does he do the same as you?"

"No" says Diane, as tears flow freely down her cheeks. It doesn't bother him. All the teachers love him anyway because he's small for his age and cute.

"Right" says Mr Glover in a very determined way. "A separate line for those who have free school meals, hey? We'll soon see about that! And you've no need to worry, Diane. As long as you have a good nutritious lunchtime meal inside you from now on, I'll not breathe a word to your parents."

Lynn then pipes up, "May I add something else, Mr Glover?"

"By all means."

"Well, Diane is not the only one who goes hungry because of the way she's treated."

"Really? Thank you for that. Leave this with me. It'll be all sorted by next Monday.

Before the end of the day the school prefects start to spread the rumour that something's afoot. Those who make coffee for the teachers before Thursday's monthly staff meeting, are told it's cancelled and on Mr Kaye's calendar it says:

"STAFF MEETING CANCELLED. INSTEAD, MEETING WITH BG - MY ROOM."

The whole school is abuzz with rumours about what's happening behind the scenes.

On Monday morning at registration, Miss Wraith announces that all those having a school meal will form one line, not two separate ones. Lynn gives Diane a knowing smile.

Meanwhile Mr Kaye, the head teacher, drives to Diane's house to post a typed letter saying,

"Dear Mr and Mrs Royston,

Mr Glover and I have discussed the educational school trip to Switzerland that's been organised by school.

Since we have one spare place to fill we both wondered whether your son, Dan, would like to fill it?

Apart from Dan's pocket money, there will be no cost – we are happy for the school-fund to be used for this.

We have come to this decision because Dan is such a pleasant, hardworking boy – popular with staff as well as his peers.

Needless to say, this letter is private and confidential and its contents will remain so.

Mr Glover and I would like to discuss this further with you and we're both available to come to your home on Wednesday, immediately after school.

Please write us a note saying whether this is convenient.

Yours sincerely,

Montague P Kaye"

"Do you know what?" says Mrs Royston to her husband "I thought I saw Mr Kaye climbing into his car outside our front garden not five minutes ago."

"What? Do you mean he's delivered the letter in person?" replies her husband, as he stands unsteadily to peer out of the front window. "I hope he doesn't think we're a charity case."

News of the letter causes great excitement for Dan but huge anxiety for Diane – until she reads its contents.

      *   *   *   *   *   *   *   *   *

Two days later, while Diane is working on the market stall, Mr Kaye and Mr Glover both arrive at the Royston household.

A couple of ex pupils on the street recognise them. The youths are shocked by their presence because no teacher has ever been seen before on the Worsbrough Common Estate.

As the teachers walk up the garden path, the first thing they notice is the beautiful state of the Royston's garden – Mrs Royston is a keen rose-grower.

Once inside, a cup of tea is served and they all discuss the whys-and-wherefores of the school trip to Switzerland.

Mr and Mrs Royston are slightly overwhelmed by the teachers' presence but they still want reassurance that their son is not being chosen for this unusual honour, out of pity.

When that reassurance is made and everyone is sworn to confidentiality, they all shake hands as the teachers leave.

Dan is beside himself with joy and so is Diane when she returns home from the market. She doesn't share it with the family but she secretly wonders whether recent events at school have contributed to her brother's good fortune? Maybe rebels do change things for the benefit of others. Anyway, whatever the reason behind this wonderful gesture, Diane's respect for her English teacher and head teacher increases massively.

In conclusion:

"A heart in a heartless world", is a well-deserved epithet for the amazing, Brian Glover.

LIVING THE DREAM

From the tender age of nine, I set my heart on becoming a professional footballer for Barnsley FC.

Playing for Manchester United or Spurs would be good fall-back positions but Oakwell is where my loyalties lie.

Five years later, in 1969, I become a regular in the successful Barnsley Boys' Under 15s team. That summer, five of the team sign apprentice professional forms at Oakwell, plus squad member, Roy Cole, who by the end of the season had become a regular in the team.

Four other first choice players - including myself - are scholars at Holgate Grammar, thus, we are automatically expected to stay on an extra year to study for O' Levels. Of these, Ian Boyle, our school captain, opts to leave 12 months early to join Barnsley. Mick Lodge and Chris Wood have other career interests but I'm very keen to sit my exams first and then sign apprentice professional forms later - if Barnsley will still have me.

This is a risky strategy because there's a chance that the early school leavers will learn so much, I'll never catch them up. However, my decision to stay on a year is unshakeable and, anyway, I can still improve by playing for the school First XI and training one evening a week at Oakwell.

Bob Parker, the Barnsley Youth Team coach, takes these sessions and I'm certain he's impressed with my attitude and performances.

Today is Tuesday 16th September 1969 and I'm at Oakwell with eleven other amateur schoolboys who've been invited down to display their skills.

It's a lovely warm evening and we're training on the pitch immediately behind the Brewery Stand. The ground is hard so I wear my rubber-moulded studs.

After a simple warm-up we do some intense fitness work culminating in shuttle sprints. It's so tough I feel my lungs will burst but I love pushing myself to the limit. Others have packed in already but not me. I'm willing to go on till I drop.

"Di ye want to do another run, Steelie?" says Bob Parker in his broad Geordie accent. I can only answer by nodding my head but just before I set off I meander over to the long grass near the perimeter wall to throw-up. After wiping the vomit from my lips I'm ready to go again.

"No, no, no" says Bob, laughing, as he turns to the other lads who're lying around, knackered. "I hope ye've all clocked this boys because that's the attitude ye need to become a professional footballer."

Bob then hands out some training bibs and we play a six-a-side game. Everything goes right for me and even though Bob says very little, I can tell he's impressed.

The following week, he's unavailable so the first team coach, Norman Rimmington, takes the session. He learns everyone's name and it feels good when the first team coach of your favourite football club, goes to all that trouble – it makes you feel special.

"I've already heard about little Ronnie Steele" he says in passing... and I think to myself, wow! This is the man who's in charge of Eric Winstanley and Pat Howard and he knows me!

By the following summer, I complete my schooling and it's time to find a job. I'm hoping Barnsley will automatically offer me a contract but they don't. Two well-known Huddersfield Town scouts who have monitored my performances playing for the school First XI, don't approached me either.

I spend a lot of time in Locke Park improving my mastery of a football because my dad says if you want to be a footballer you must be able to make a ball "sit up and beg like the legendary Jimmy Baxter could". On one occasion I have a group around me which includes Carl Ashton and David Buttle (Bub). The challenge is to see how many times I can juggle a ball using only my feet, thighs, chest and head, before I lose control and drop it. I wear my sneakers and get the leather football down to the correct pressure because juggling a soft football on a warm day makes the task marginally easier. As I perform the kick-ups I count aloud while Carl and Bub witness that there's no cheating.

When I reach a thousand, my next goal is to beat my record of 1, 449 and when that target's passed I go for 2,000, then 3,000 and then I begin to wonder whether it'll be possible to reach 5,000? However, when I actually pass the 4,000 mark, the muscles on the outside of both shins begin to ache like mad. I've no idea how long I've been at it but after starting by the concrete-clad wall, near Kerry Hall Road, I'm now nearer the middle if the field beside the old bonfire patch. When I reach 4,990, I start shouting every kick out, aloud.

"Ninety-one, ninety-two, ninety-three, ninety-four, ninety-five, ninety-six, ninety-seven, ninety-eight, ninety-nine, Five thousand!" and I let the ball drop to the grass.

None of us can believe it. In fact after this, Bub mentions this feat every time I bump into him:

"I'll never forget that day in Locke Park, Ronnie Steele" he always says.

During the World Cup in June I finally get a message from the Barnsley manager, Jock Steele (no relation). He wants me to do a six week trial where I'll be training and playing with the Youth Team and Reserves in friendly matches.

The Wilson and Longbottom Foundry also offers me an engineering apprenticeship at this time but I decline it at the last minute on the basis that I would have made a lousy engineer, anyway. Only the trade union side of things would have really appealed to me.

Consequently, by 'burning my boats', it's now more important than ever that I impress the football coaches at Oakwell and get an apprentice professional contract.

My height and weight are still a concern.

"Now tell iz, Ronnie, what's yer father like?" asks Bob Parker, in the final week of my trial.

"What's my father like? What do you mean, Bob?" I reply.

"Well, is he tall, short, slim, muscular?"

"He's short and slim but very strong" I say.

"Hmmm, that means we'll hev ti work on ye in the gymnasium now that we're ganna sign ye."

"What? You're going to sign me? Really? You're not joking? I say.

"Why naa, I'm not joking. The thing that swung it for me was when ye were on the bench for the Reserves at Guiseley. Di ye remember? I asked ye if ye'd play for me on the right wing and ye said ye'd play anywhere as long as ye got on the pitch" says Bob. "Well that clinched it for me."

The following day, my dad and I walk down to Oakwell to discuss terms and sign the contract; and as we make our way on Eldon Street he tells me this story about a friend of his at his previous colliery:

One day at the start of his shift, his workmate said,

"Have you heard about our Tommy, Fred. They've signed him on at Oakwell. He's going to be a footballer. What do you think to that then? Our Tommy, a footballer!"

"And who was your workmate, Dad?" I ask.

"Why, it was Tommy Taylor's uncle who was also called Tommy, and I now know exactly how he felt" says Dad.

In the manager's office at Oakwell, I'm a little disappointed with the offer of only a one-year contract. I'm even more disheartened with the £6 and 10 shillings a week I'll be paid because it's ten shillings less than what the other apprentices are receiving. However, as the club secretary points out, I've got to take cognisance of the fact that the others are already in their second year.

My first game is as sub for the Reserves away at The River Lane ground in Retford. I feel very excited because it's only a few weeks since I was a school pupil and now I'm one of two substitutes playing for Barnsley Reserves. Then I discover the Oakwell custom is for the subs to carry the team kit from the coach to the ground.

I find this a bit humiliating, so from that day forth, I'm determined to try and make sure I'm always first choice for the team.

However, today I have to help carry the kit - kept in a heavy wicker basket - down a long winding path to the ground. At the entrance there's about half a dozen young autograph hunters waving books and pens.

We have a couple of first teamers playing today but the youngsters are also hoping to collect the signatures of future stars.

I can't believe it. It doesn't seem two minutes since I was harvesting the signatures of footballers, myself. Now it's me who's signing. If my old school mates could see me now!

However, living the dream doesn't last long because the following Monday morning we begin the working day with nearly two hours light training, and in the afternoon we're given chores.

These are the usual afternoon jobs we have to do in a typical week:

Monday pm: Boot-cleaning, litter picking from the terraces or divoting (divoting is when you replace chunks of turf that have been gouged out of the playing surface by players' studs).

Tuesday pm: Sweeping and mopping the changing rooms and corridor.

Wednesday pm: Big clean, including players baths/showers and fans' toilets in preparation for that evening's match.

Thursday pm: I spend every Thursday afternoon studying for more O' Levels at Barnsley College. My colleagues have divoting duties or litter picking again.

Friday pm: An hour's cleaning, then the afternoon free.

These tasks create a debate at home.

"It's nothing but cheap labour" says my dad. "Imagine how much more expensive it would be if the club employed adult workers. It'd cost them three or four times more."

"True" I reply "but the team coaches and the club are keen to instil good values and habits while we're young. Anyway, Bob Parker is a man of integrity."

My mam says, "If that's what footballers like Best, Law and Charlton had to do, Fred, then perhaps it's a good grounding. Many would give their eye teeth for such an opportunity."

During the first few weeks in the job, I have a bit of a hard time because I'm the only new apprentice and I go through a tough initiation period. My mates have all changed since their school days because they've had a year to get used to the dressing-room banter and clever put-downs. And it's at this time I realise that the 'thick professional footballer' is a myth. They might not be all Einsteins but they do tend to be sharp-witted and spatially gifted – meaning they have eyes in the back of their heads.

I also soon discover that some lads are helpful but others test me out to see how far they can push me. The worst are the insecure apprentices who see my success as a danger to theirs. Consequently, in this dog-eat-dog environment, if you can't stand up for yourself you'll quickly flounder. I put up with it for so long, then I've had enough.

One Friday afternoon, all the apprentices are sitting in the away dressing-room ready to change for home. Big Jimmy Curran (not his real name) and I are cleaning the showers by hosing down the tiles. When I look round, most of the other lads have poked their heads around the door, smiling, so I know something's afoot. Suddenly I feel the hose being turned on me by Jimmy and he's laughing his socks off. I'm in my training gear, soaked head to foot.

That's it! He's gone too far and I'm ready to do battle no matter how big he is. So I walk into the dressing room, pick up all of Jimmy's clothes from his peg and dump them down into the puddle by the circular grate.

There's silence for a couple of seconds, then...

"What the f**k are tha laiking* at, Steelie? I've to go home in these" he bawls, picking them up from the shower floor. "Look at 'em, they're dripping wet through. You f**king lunatic."

"Think yourself lucky I didn't hit you round your fu*king head with this tin mop-bucket!" I shout, grabbing hold of the handle and lifting it aloft. "I nearly did."

Jimmy must see the fire in my eyes because he backs down from a scrap.

"Bloody hell. Did you see that? That was nifty" says Graham Collingwood, and 'Nifty Norris' becomes my nickname*.

From that day forth, Jimmy Curran becomes a silent enemy and it is me who becomes the chief dressing room teaser, yet I never let it descend into bullying. In fact, quite the opposite.

I'm two weeks into my apprenticeship and my star is beginning to rise, slowly but surely.

On the football side of my job, things are progressing nicely. There's still a belief in the 1970s that you've either got it or you haven't, and if you haven't got it – tough! I don't agree because my strongly held opinion is that most people can develop skills if they work on them often enough. Therefore, with this in mind, I set out to improve. I see one of the senior players catching the ball on the back of his neck and think that's something I'd love to do. So I spend hours on it until it's well and truly mastered. However, although this might make me appear more talented, it doesn't improve my ability in a game, one jot. It's just a way of showing off.

Then, six weeks into my apprenticeship, Bob Parker identifies a few things about my game that will make a big difference and sits me down for a chat.

"Aa'll give it to ye straight, Nifty" says Bob, "Ye must purron mair weight and muscle, improve yer tacklin' and change yer attitude from being too nice."

That's just what I want to hear because I'm certain it's the magic key that will help me improve faster than anyone else.

Bob provides me with time for extra weight training and after a few weeks, although my muscles haven't expanded, my strength has improved enormously.

I'm still a very poor eater and anyway my mam can't afford best steak every day on the £4 a week board I give her.

There's still that dressing room jealousy from a few individuals who're quick to label someone a 'creep' if they stay behind for extra practice. Thus, I spend as much time as possible on Shawland's soccer pitch near my home, developing my skills. Sometimes I work alone but often I'm accompanied by my mate, Carl.

I soon start to master the slide tackle and with my added strength and ruthlessness, tackling becomes a feature of my game. In one match at the Shay against Halifax town, I become a bit too brutal and Bob tells me off in front of the other players for going over the top.

"For f**ksake, Nifty. If aa'd been reffing ye'd hev been sent straight off, man."

I love to watch some of the new players and copy their skills. Norman Dean does this fancy back heel that I've never seen before and soon I'm performing it in games. A young Scottish lad called Alistair Miller is able to do with a football what no other player can do, so I spend hours trying to copy him. It feels great when I'm able to perform some of the magic that senior stars are well-known for.

It's not always onwards and upwards, though, because after one bad Under 19s defeat, the manager, Johnny Steele has us in his office, one at a time, for a 'right bollocking'.

He doesn't half upset me when he says: "Ronnie Steele, if you'd played like that during your trial period, I wouldn't have signed you."

I leave his office feeling deflated and reluctant to tell my mates but it's not long before I learn that he's said virtually the same thing to us all.

Towards the end of my first season I'm picked to play for the Reserves against Hull at Boothferry Park and I'm still only 16. For another Reserve game at Oakwell, I'm substitue and I overhear the ex Everton player, Billy Brindle, talking to Bob Parker.

"You wanna keep your eye on young Ronnie Steele. He's got some future that lad. He just reminds me of Alan Ball at Goodison - same never-say-die attitude."

"Ye don't have to tell *me* that" replies Bob Parker.

Then I cough loudly as I appear from around the corner and enter the dug-out. They've no idea I've been eavesdropping. I suddenly feel all light-headed, like a balloon filled with helium. That's two people who've likened me to Alan Ball: Barry Hines and Billy Brindle. My God! And Billy Brindle should know, he's trained alongside the great Alan Ball for years at Goodison Park.

That evening I mention it to my dad.

"Ah, well, don't let it go to your head. You're only as good as your last game. You need to make your weak foot as cultured as your left" he says, and I feel it in my bones that this is prudent advice.

A couple of weeks before my 17th birthday, the manager invites me into his office again to say he's pleased to offer me a further one-year extension on my contract. This is with a view to signing me on full-time professional forms at the end of it next season if my progress is satisfactory. There's also a pay rise of 50p a week.

When my first season finally ends, we have a couple of weeks off and then return to prepare the Oakwell pitch for the following season with our grounds men, Albert Brookes and his assistant, Terry. It means some heavy work, riddling tonnes of soil and then wheel barrowing it into an enormous shed. Later, the fine soil is used to re-seed large areas of the pitch. We also give a fresh lick of paint to some areas of the ground.

To prevent boredom we listen to Jimmy Young's Show on the radio and take it in turns to sing along. *Sweet Caroline, Knock Three Times* and *Brown Sugar* become our favourite songs.

The final close-season task is an unforeseen one. Our training pitch, the Queens Ground, has been out of service for a year or two because of subsidence. The NCB has to spend thousands repairing the damage but by the summer of 1971 it should be ready to train on. Except, there's another problem - the top-soil contains tens of thousands of small stones the size of Maltesers, which have risen to the surface. To exacerbate matters, the travelling community has allowed their horses onto the pitch while the ground was soft. Now, it's rock hard and covered in deep hoof prints that are filled with, hard-to-dislodge, stones.

Paul Turner and I are assigned the task of sweeping up every single one. Paul is methodical. He isolates a five feet wide margin, just inside the touchline, using string and metal tent pegs. When that 100 yards strip has been completely cleared of stones, then the adjacent strip is isolated and swept, and so on, ad nauseum.

"What did we do to deserve this mindless task, Paul?" I ask, as I sweep another pile of stones onto his shovel.

"I don't know, Nifty" he replies, "but hard labour for convicts can't be as boring as this."

It's an awful task, but eventually we get rid of all the stones and fill in the divots with soil and seed until the pitch is as smooth as a bowling green.

I've thoroughly enjoyed the footballing side of the past twelve months and I've made a couple of really good friends: Brian 'Smigger' Smith from Lundwood and Graham Collingwood from Minsthorpe. Just being in the presence of these lads is great fun.

During the close season I'm still working on my game every spare minute I can find. I practise with Carl, shooting and dribbling, and it's not time wasted because it comes in very useful when the new season begins.

My personal self-confidence has flourished, partly because I now realise I can learn faster than most. Furthermore, at the start of the season I rated myself fourteenth out of fourteen apprentices. Now, I believe I'm possibly the ninth best in the group.

However, 'living the dream' has its downside: I don't mind hard work but I'm certain some of our labouring duties are about the Club saving money.

Moreover, the short term contracts mean you're in a constant state of worry about your future.

* Laiking is a local word meaning playing.

** Years later when I bump into my old colleagues from Oakwell they always use my old nickname. "Hiya Nifty" they'll say. "How's life treating you?"

Ronnie Steele

POLITICS IN THE DRESSING ROOM

It's autumn 1971 and the Troubles in Northern Ireland are escalating. One hundred people have already been killed and British soldiers begin to destroy roads between the Republic and Northern Ireland as a security measure. The same soldiers, who were first welcomed into the province to protect the Catholic population, are now perceived as taking the side of the Protestants.

The John Lennon classic, *Imagine* and Don McLean's *American Pie* have captured the imagination of millions of music lovers.

Meanwhile, Barnsley FC manager, Johnny Steele, resigns and takes on an admin job at the club. The 40 year old Scot, John McSeveney, becomes our new manager.

All the players and staff at the club are nervous, wondering what Mr McSeveney will be like and whether our faces will fit under the new regime. Everyone is relieved that he'll continue with Norman Rimmington as chief coach and Bob Parker as Youth and Reserve team coach. From what we can discover, John McSeveney's football pedigree as a backroom employee, seems fairly modest but even the top managers have to start somewhere. He's a short, fast-talking Glaswegian with an accent not dissimilar to Bill Shankly's and a quick wit to match.

All the apprentice footballers are given a pay rise of 50p now that the UK's gone decimal, which brings my weekly wage up to a magnificent £7. All my mates from school who work in industry tell me they're paid more than that. However, I'm now not the lowest paid in the club, but it's still a matter of a tanner looking down on a threepenny bit.

I'm making excellent progress on the football pitch under our new boss. All the many hours I've spent, during the summer, shooting and dribbling, have not been wasted.

Against Sheffield Wednesday Under 19s away, I'm up against one of the Owls' greatest prospects, Jimmy Mullen, and straight after the game the Barnsley director, Mr Potter JP, is eager to congratulate me. This is very unusual and I know exactly what's excited him. I've perfected another, Aly Millar, dribbling trick and I'm feeling cock-a-hoop.

This is followed by a series of very satisfying performances away at Huddersfield Town, Hull City, Scunthorpe United and at home to Newcastle United. I'm also hitting great shots from distance and scoring the occasional screamer*. My goal away at Huddersfield Town is the best of my professional career so far. From a headed pass by Alan Hopkinson, I convert a sweet half-volley from 20 yards. It's also pleasing that my goal is witnessed by our new manager, which will do my reputation no harm at all.

It's at this time that Bob Parker accidentally comes across a very clever motivational trick. One morning a mysterious pair of giant white bloomers turn up in the dressing room. On the back, written in giant letters, it says,

"W*NKER"

Where they have come from? Nobody knows. Who's placed them there? Nobody knows. Tommy Meehan, our goalkeeper, is a bit of a comic and decides to model them for all to see.

"I wonder what Bob Parker will make of these?" asks 'Rock' Boyle, smiling.

"Bob'll find it hilarious" replies 'Sammy' Senior who's always up for a bit of mischief. "Have we to put it to the test?" he asks, laughing.

We walk from the stand to the training pitch as a group, with Tommy surrounded on all sides and hidden. As we set off on our warm-up, we split up and Tommy and his giant knickers are exposed for Bob to see.

Sammy was right. Bob's doubled-up laughing but when Tommy tries taking them off, Bob stops him.

"Hey, Tommy. Ye've no need to take them off. Ye can wear them for the rest of the session, man" says Bob, and the rest of the players whoop and cheer.

From that day onwards, the w*nker shorts are awarded each day to the worst player, who then has to wear them for the next session. It works well. No one is pleased to be awarded them, so it does act as an extra incentive to train hard. However, Bob's careful to make sure everyone gets a turn to wear them, and the light-hearted element is maintained.

By late October, it's plain to see that the First Team is doing badly. If they continue in this vein it could mean relegation to the Fourth Division. I'm extremely worried because I'm not just an employee, I'm a dyed-in-the-wool, Reds fanatic.

At about this time I start to have a problem with my right knee. It swells up after each game, so I'm sent to the empty referee's changing room for treatment. I have to sit on the edge of the bath and run cold water over it for five minutes, using the hosepipe, and then do the same with very hot water. The treatment lasts about an hour. I'm sitting there alone, with no one to talk to, bored out of my skull.

Our coaches, Norman and Bob, who also double as physios, explain that the use of hot and cold water is the best way to treat a swelling. I continue with my labouring duties in the afternoon, though, because they don't seem to worsen my injury. However, a pattern is definitely emerging: the water treatment reduces the swelling, and by Friday of each week I'm pronounced fit for the Saturday game. Then the same cycle is repeated – play, treatment, recover; play, treatment, recover...

As winter approaches and the pitches get softer I seem to get less trouble from my knee and my performances continue to improve.

As we're sitting in the dressing room before our next game against Doncaster Rovers Reserves, Bob Parker says as part of his pre match pep talk:

"Just gi' the ball to Nifty on the edge of the area. He's got the best shot in the Club, yer know."

Wow! I can't believe what I've just heard. The best shot in the Club, indeed! Once again I feel slightly giddy and I'm not sure whether it's the smell of the liniment or the praise that's made me lightheaded. I suspect Bob's exaggerating but at least his comment means I'm getting noticed.

A few weeks before Christmas I'm picked for the Reserves to play the First Team on the Queens Ground training pitch and I've another chance to impress. My robust tackling has caught the eye, so today I'm going to give them something to talk about. However, it turns out I'm a bit too wild in my challenges again and I get the Barnsley right back, Dave Booth, in a bone-crunching tackle. He limps away looking very annoyed.

In the dressing room later I get a message from Dave via another apprentice.

"Dave Booth says he's going to break your f**king leg if you ever tackle him like that again."

"Oh he does, does he?" I say, slapping my wet towel down hard on the floor. "Well you can just go and tell Dave f**king Booth that he's... probably got a good point really and I do apologise."

The whole changing room's in uproar.

Actually, I'm not too pleased with myself for upsetting Dave because he's a really nice guy and I've been a big fan of his since I was at school.

Nevertheless, my general confidence continues to rise, especially when I realise I can make people laugh.

In the New Year, the First Team is continuing to under-perform and now there's serious concern we'll be relegated.

Moreover, there's personal, financial trouble on the horizon, which impinges on my professional career – and it's all of my own making. My father is a mineworker and he and his colleagues are on a collision course with the Tory government.

My dad has all the arguments over the industrial dispute at his fingertips.

"I'm much worse off than I was ten years ago" says Dad, as he sips his tea. "In 1960 the British miners were at the top of the earnings league for industrial workers. Now we're way, way down."

"Are you certain about that then Dad?" I ask.

"Certain? Certain? Here, just study this" and he passes me a copy of the NUM newspaper with a graph to prove his point.

On 9th January 1972 the miners go on all out national strike for the first time since the General Strike of 1926.

Towards the end of the month, as the strike begins to bite, my dad agrees to go picketing throughout East Anglia. Their chief aim is to stop the import of foreign coal through the East Anglia docks. The flying pickets are put-up in digs and on university campuses.

As a family, things get very tough for us. My mam's earning £5 a week as a part-time cleaner and I'm bringing in my measly £6.50 now (after the insurance stamp is deducted).

"What kind of a bloke is John McSeveney?" asks my mam as I get ready for Oakwell one morning.

"I don't think he's the type of boss to get close to his players" I say, as I put my snap in my bag.

"Do you think he'll be one to support the miners' cause?

"I don't really know. Why do you ask, mam?" I say.

"I was just wondering... do you think there's any mileage in asking for a pay rise because of our circumstances?" says Mam.

"Hmmm, I never thought of that. Might be worth a try. They don't pay us enough, anyway" I reply.

That morning, before training, I make an appointment to see Mr McSeveney after I've finished my work duties. His office is under the main stand at the top of the players' tunnel. I have to walk from the home dressing room, past the Treatment Room - where Norman Rimmington and Bob Parker are dealing with injured players. I stop outside the Gaffer's office to compose myself. There are no windows or natural light in this corridor. A strip light above me illuminates a red door with a sign:

MANAGER

Mr J H McSeveney

The old plastic sign bearing Johnny Steele's name has been prised off and this new one stuck in its place.

I knock and wait. Nothing. I knock again.

"Come in!"

I sit down on a chair opposite the gaffer with his desk between us. There's the smell of smoke and half a cigar in an ashtray. The frosted window behind him allows bright sunlight to stream through. It's quite dazzling.

"What's the problem?" he says.

I shuffle forward in my chair and clear my throat nervously.

"Well it's like this. My dad's on strike, my mam's in a very low paid job and I'm taking home £6.50 a week. So, I was wondering whether you'd consider increasing my wage by 50p a week."

"So let me get this straight. Your father's on strike which means there's a reduced income in your household and you want the club to make up for the shortfall" says McSeveney as he uses his hand to adjust his comb-over. "Is that it?"

Hmmm... This is not going as well as I had hoped, and I could have sworn there was a slight scoff in his voice.

"Well I wouldn't quite put it like that. I think my pay is too little and an extra 50p a week won't break the club but it will help me and my family enormously."

"Perhaps your father would have been wiser not to have come out on strike" says Mr McSeveney.

It takes all my powers of self-discipline not to react with a, "My dad's not a scab, Mr McSeveney."

After a few more exchanges, the boss says, "Hmmm... give me some time to think about it." So I thank him, get up and leave.

On my way back down the corridor, I try to assess how the meeting went and I'm not too comfortable with it. Mr McSeveney's comments weren't supportive of our family predicament, so I'm not optimistic about the outcome.

That evening I recount the meeting to my mother.

Next day, after training, the PFA Union representative, Norman Dean, takes me to one side and says,

"Do me a favour Nifty, will you? I need these new laces putting in my boots. Would you come to the boot room and sort it out for me?"

Norman's a decent guy. I always clean his boots and every so often he puts a ten-bob note in my hand as a thank you.

In the boot room, Norman picks up one of his Adidas boots and examines it. It's shining so beautifully, he can almost see his reflection.

"Actually, Nifty, I don't really want you to re-lace my boots, I just want to tip you the wink about something. The gaffer seems to think it's a big joke that you've asked for a pay rise because your father's on strike" he tells me. "He's now going round telling all and sundry about a meeting you had with him. Now, I'm going to give you a bit of advice: Always approach me first if you're not happy about your pay and conditions. That's what I was elected for."

"Is the Gaffer really telling everyone about our private meeting?" I ask. "That's not fair! That's not right!" and I head off to confront McSeveney.

"Whoa back, Young 'un!" shouts Norman. "Give yourself some time to calm down. If you want to complain, we'll go and see him together, maybe tomorrow. In the meantime, jot down on a piece of paper, the date of your meeting and everything that was said. You never know when you'll need it."

When I reach the dressing room, some of the first teamers have left for a game of golf but a few are sat in a corner talking to the gaffer. I'm quite surprised to see him in the dressing room. Up to now he's not really mixed with his players.

'Smigger' and I take our buckets and mops through the room to fill them up with hot water and detergent. Suddenly, all conversation stops and there's silence.

Norman Dean follows us in and sits two or three places away from Mr McSeveney.

"You know, Ronnie, you shouldn't be taken-in by all these bleeding-heart stories about how badly off the miners are. It's not true" says the gaffer.

I'm tempted to say, "How the hell would you know?" but I know I'd be asking for trouble.

Norman is looking at me and shaking his head, as though to say, don't let him draw you.

"On the contrary" I reply - ignoring everything Norman's told me - "In 1960 the British miners were at the top of the earnings league for industrial workers. Now they're way, way down."

"Yes but working in the pit is not like it used to be, you know. It's all mechanised now. It's easy compared to what it used to be" says the gaffer.

Norman is still shaking his head.

"Maybe conditions have improved" I argue "but nevertheless, working underground in the dark with all that dust and filth in the atmosphere is not something that I'd choose to do."

I look at the first teamers and they're now staring at the floor.

Then the gaffer says, "Just look at the pay rise these miners are after. It's ridiculous. They'll be paid nearly as much as doctors if they win this dispute."

Norman's still shaking his head and his eyes have widened.

"Well perhaps the gap between industrial workers and the very well paid, should be less" I tell him, standing my ground.

"Whooo, get you!" replies the boss. "You're beginning to sound like a proper communist, Ronnie."

Norman Dean has heard enough. He can feel the dressing room temperature rising and decides he must intervene.

"When you've a minute, boss, I'd like a private word."

The boss walks towards the exit door with Norman Dean following. I suspect Norman's no idea what he's going to say to him but he feels he just has to change the subject, somehow.

I realise I've opened my big mouth too much, but I was provoked. Mr McSeveney has betrayed a trust and as a consequence, I've lost respect.

When I get home I'm still annoyed by what's happened. My mother, like all mothers, can sense there's something wrong.

"Come on, what's up?"

So I explain what's happened while it's fresh in my mind.

Then she says,

"Working down a mine is easy, is it? I bet McSeveney's never done a proper day's work in his life. Anyway, you did right to say what you did. Never stand for the egg under the hat, that's my motto. And the sooner you get away from that place the better."

"You're joking, Mam. Leave Barnsley Football Club? I'd sooner gouge out my eyes with a rusty spoon" I say, as I switch on the news to find out the latest on the strike.

A few weeks later on 28th February the Tory government accepts defeat and the miners win a substantial pay increase.

I doubt John McSeveney is celebrating the outcome; certainly not like my family is, anyway.

Henceforth, if his name crops up in conversation at home, John McSeveney is never referred to by his proper name. If we allude to him at all, it's as The Snake.

Despite my political differences with him, my performances keep improving and at 17 I'm playing more regularly for the reserves. The attendances for Reserve matches are fairly poor – maybe a few hundred – but the noise the fans make when I score a goal is deafening compared to anything I've experienced before.

"I wonder what it's like scoring for the first team when there's a crowd of 10,000" I say to Graham Collingwood.

"It might be something you'll soon find out if you keep scoring like that, Nifty" he replies.

But as the pitches firm up in March my nagging knee injury returns. I'm back into the cycle of play, treatment, play, but my condition is deteriorating.

On April 14th I finish a Reserve match against Halifax Town at Oakwell but I'm in great discomfort.

This turns out to be my final professional game, ever, and the very last time I walk on the Oakwell turf. I have to throw on the sick and it takes physiotherapy, a major operation and 20 months of remedial therapy before I can get back up to 50% fitness.

To add insult to injury the First Team have a disastrous end to the season and are relegated to the Division Four.

I'm devastated.

My political experience as an apprentice footballer, has a profound effect on my whole outlook. For the rest of my life I know, for a certainty, which side of the political divide I am on.

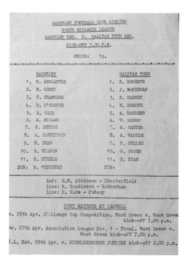

LETTING GO OF THE DREAM

This long-term knee injury is a terrible nuisance. Dr Duggan, the club doctor, can't diagnose the problem so I'm sent to see consultant surgeon, Mr Bhadreshwar. He recommends physiotherapy but when that fails he books me in for surgery. The problem, he says, could be cartilage deterioration.

I'm soon operated on. Three days later, Mr Bhadreshwar visits everyone in the ward to give them post-op feedback.

He's straight to the point.

"I looked inside your knee and found the medial meniscus torn posteriorly. I removed the cartilage and discovered early changes of osteo-arthritis. Therefore, you must immediately forget all about having a career in professional football. This is important, no more professional football." Then he's off to talk to his next patient.

I'm too stunned to speak.

What did Mr Bhadreshwar say? Have I heard him correctly? Did he say, forget all about playing professional football? I want him to repeat it or, better still, tell me not to be so bloody stupid and that a full recovery is expected.

"Excuse me! Excuse me!" I shout "I don't understand. I need to ask more... "

But I might as well talk to the wall. The consultant and all his young disciples are now focussed on the elderly man in the last bed. Like all consultants at this time, Mr Bhadreshwar is far too busy to waste valuable time repeating or explaining things fully.

I turn over in bed, put my face in the pillow, and sob.

Two young nurses are left to keep an eye on me for the rest of the day. A screen is drawn around my bed and I'm given two tablets. I don't even ask what they're for. I drift in and out of sleep for hours until visiting time.

That evening my mam and dad arrive but they're ambushed by the Ward Sister. After a few minutes discussion they're led in to see me. I'm determined not to weep but when I see both of them with red swollen eyes, it's more than I can cope with.

I try to reassure *them* that everything will turn out all right in the end but the words just won't come out.

"I'll, uh, be, uh, okay, mam" is all I manage to say before I have to bury my face in my hands. Next day, word has reached everyone on the ward and those who are able to get out of bed, come to try and cheer me up. This includes five young fellows who have serious renal problems.

They're all so kind and funny, I soon forget my own woes. When they leave me I feel much better.

Later, one of the nurses assigned to me, confides that my new friends have all got a very poor prognosis, themselves. I didn't realise how serious renal failure is. This helps me put things into perspective and for the first time I glimpse the idea that not playing football does not necessarily mean the end of the world. Perhaps there is life after football.

As my injury was sustained in a Reserve Team fixture as an apprentice professional, I qualify for financial compensation. The amount on offer is the same whether you are an international star like George Best or an apprentice, like me. When I receive the cheque from the PFA, the blow is softened and I'm even more relieved when I'm also awarded an extra weekly financial allowance for the rest of my life to, augment my income. The ridiculous thing is, I'm now receiving 50% more than many of the young full-time professionals at Oakwell.

This compensation finances my career-switch to teaching.

Furthermore, the English Football Association very generously offer post-career support. They finance my first football coaching qualification and also pay for me a fortnight's residential coaching course in Durham.

I do miss playing football everyday, and the camaraderie of the dressing room. Nevertheless, I certainly don't miss the lack of security or the scandalously low pay of professional football.

In 1974, just before I leave my home town for teacher training college, I go to visit my old colleagues at Oakwell.

Bob Parker tells me he's resigning as assistant coach and his job will be advertised soon. I'm shocked. Bob is a man of wisdom and integrity and will be a huge loss to the Club.

"Ye should apply for my job, Nifty" says Bob.

I chuckle and say, "You flatter me Bob, but I've no intention of ever committing myself to an insecure, short term contract, again – if I can help it.

Four years later, when I begin teaching at Kexborough Junior, I still have a recurring dream where I'm sitting in the Oakwell changing room before a big match. I can smell the liniment, sense the atmosphere and picture Bob Parker giving his usual pep talk.

Letting go of the dream is not easy but the support I get smoothes the way nicely.

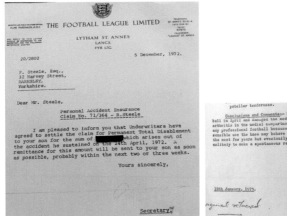

THE GREAT WESTERN POP FESTIVAL

It's Thursday 25th May 1972 and me and my mates are getting ready for the Great Western Pop Festival at Bardney near Lincoln.

There are at least 10 guys who are going from Barnsley, and we're all good pals. Carl Ashton and I are hitch-hiking there and meeting up with the rest when we reach the festival site.

The short term weather forecast is bleak.

Neither Carl nor I have a tent but he's confident we'll find shelter somewhere if the weather deteriorates. We each carry a rucksack with a few spare clothes, snacks and a rolled up sleeping bag.

I air my worries about the weather.

"Once we get soaked we'll never get dry again, you know."

"I've 'roughed it' all over England and I've never once failed to find shelter in an emergency" replies Carl, glancing up at the threatening clouds. There's always some church doorway or nearby bridge to shelter under."

"And you do realise we'll not be welcomed by the local population, don't you, Carl? They'll treat us like tramps" I say.

"Well, what's up with that?" he replies. "We can take it. And remember, sleeping rough didn't do George Orwell any harm. In fact it turned him into a world-famous author."

"Aye, but it also gave him TB."

By 1:30 in the afternoon we get dropped off just north of Lincoln by a travelling salesman. Although the clouds still look menacing and the air feels damp, it's not yet rained. We continue to cadge lifts to Bardney which is about 10 miles east of Lincoln, and as we walk, we talk.

I love to hear Carl's stories about his previous adventures in Blackpool with Phil Parker, when they slept in derelict hotels and bathed in the sun and the Irish Sea. I ask him about his trip to the Isle of Wight Pop Festival of 1970 and he waxes lyrical.

"It was simply the best time of my life. We saw The Who, the Moody Blues, Hendrix, Ralph McTell, Free, Procol Harum and dozens of others at the top of their game. You couldn't move, it was so packed with music-lovers.

"I wish I could have been there to see The Who" I tell him wistfully.

It takes us six hours to hitchhike from Barnsley to the eastern side of Lincoln but the time just flies by. I'm suffering a bit of knee-pain but I'm so excited I hardly notice it.

"The line-up tomorrow is exciting" says Carl. There's the Beach Boys and..."

A red VW van has just passed us and the driver applies the brakes, then reverses to pick us up.

Out he climbs and asks: "You lads wouldn't be heading for the Festival, would you?"

"Yeah!"

"Get in then. That's where I'm going." And he slides open his side door and we climb in the back and sit on the floor beside some boxes.

"You're not an artiste are you?" Carl asks.

"No. No such luck. I'm just the delivery man with 10 gross of sandwiches for the vendors. Help yourself to one."

Carl talks about the bands and individuals who will be performing in the next four days.

"I'm looking forward to the final night more than any other" says he. "There's Status Quo, Don McClean, Genesis and the fabulous Joe Cocker. I can't wait."

I pull my ticket out of my rucksack.

"It says here that on Sunday there's Monty Python's doing some comedy sketches, Slade, Lindisfarne, Spencer Davis and the Beach Boys and others performing. What a line up that is!"

Our driver pulls up at the entrance to a field.

"He we are boys. Enjoy yourselves and keep out of trouble. Sure you don't want a sarney?"

"No thanks, but we do appreciate the lift."

There's a large meadow in front of us with hundreds of young people milling about. Evenly spaced within two adjacent fields are five enormous marquees – nearly as big as the circus tent that comes to the Queens Ground every year.

"These, Ronnie, are our digs for the next four nights" announces Carl, as a sudden gust of arctic wind forces him to raise his coat collar. "In the meantime, why don't we explore the village?"

Halfway between the festival site and the village, it begins to rain. Each of us has a large piece of polythene in our rucksacks with a hole cut in the middle to put our head through – rather like a poncho. We look ridiculous but they keep us bone-dry except for the bottom part of our jeans.

The wind, I notice, is getting stronger.

The village is fairly deserted but those residents who are out, look daggers at us, which is hardly surprising given the bad press there's been. Maybe they think we're here to mug them in the street or steal the family silver.

After walking round for a bit, we come across an old church with folk stood outside giving out leaflets and getting soaked. The vicar hands me one and says:

"You're welcome to come inside and enjoy a free sandwich and hot drink. You can even dry your wet clothes as well."

So Carl and I change into our dry jeans behind the church pews and put the wet ones on the radiators. The Bovril is very much appreciated and after an hour we pack our dried jeans, thank the church-goers, and set off walking back to the festival site. It's stopped raining now but the wind is so strong it's blowing dustbins and litter all over the street. A dead branch flies past us, just above our heads.

"Bloody hell" says Carl. "Did you see that? I feel like an extra in Macbeth."

 When we reach the field with the marquees, it's getting dark but we can just make out that only three of them are still standing. The other two have been flattened. By the time we've entered one of the remaining tents, we hear that yet another has blown down.

The marquee we choose to sleep in is as packed as Blackpool beach on a hot Bank Holiday Monday. We tiptoe around and over bodies to get a decent place because no one wants to kip near the draughty doorway. Then I hear familiar accents and laughter. It's our Barnsley mates.

We sit down beside them about three yards from the centre pole that's holding up the roof. There's an unusual smell coming from behind us.

"Smell that? That's shit" says Ged, climbing into his sleeping bag and laying his head on his rucksack.

"Shit?"

"Yeah" says Ged. "You know, marijuana."

I turn my head to see a guy with long hair and untidy beard, sucking on a weird looking pipe. He's lighting it with a taper and, judging by his glazed eyes, he's well gone. The taper sets fire to his hair but is quickly doused by his two friends.

I retch. There's nothing I detest more than the stench of burning hair. It's miles worse than marijuana.

Inside the marquee there's quite a pleasant party atmosphere but the greatest noise is coming from a group of Hari Krishna supporters who keep ringing bells and tiny cymbals whilst gently chanting,

"Hari Krishna, Hari Krishna, Hari Krishna, Hari Krishna" over and over again.

All the lads agree that it sounds wonderfully spiritual but after a while it gets a trifle tiresome.

"Don't they know anymore words?" shouts Ralph? But no one answers.

"Ey up" he says to one of the singers. "Are there any more words to your song?"

"This song's a mantra. It frees your mind. No more words" says the Asian guy with the shaven head and orange sari.

I'm enjoying the exchange but Steve Wathey is tugging on my arm, keen to tell me something:

"Ronnie! Ronnie! They say this is the last marquee standing. All the others..."

However, I'm struggling to hear Steve because Ralph has added his own lyrics to the chant.

"Harry Ramsden, Harry Ramsden, Harry Ramsden, Harry Ramsden." And the rest of us we can't sing along for laughing.

As I climb into my sleeping bag, I notice the central mast, almost as thick as a telegraph pole, is making the most frightful, creaking sound.

"Ey up, Carlos. You don't think that bloody great pole's going to collapse on top of us, do you?"

"Nah. Safe as houses. Wish our house was as safe" he replies; and on the word 'safe' we hear an almighty crack and crunch and the pole starts to topple over, landing on top of scores of people. We find we're suddenly cast into the open air and the blackness of the night, with the gale-force wind lashing our faces. It feels like we've been shipwrecked and it's every man for himself.

"Quick!" shouts Carl. "Let's tear off some..."

But I can't hear him properly because the canvass is flapping and cracking like a whiplash. Carl's pulling on a piece of canvass so I help him. We manage to tear off two pieces, each a bit bigger than a double blanket. Thank God it's not raining! Now what? Everyone's scattered except the hippy, smoking the peace pipe. He's still in a stupor, oblivious to all the drama around him. Our other mates have disappeared.

We drag the canvases, sleeping bags and rucksacks, to the edge of the field where there's a protective hedge and dry ditch. We trample down one bit of canvas to use as a ground sheet. Then, climbing into our sleeping bags, we pull the other canvas on top of us to keep us. This canvas material isn't like ordinary tent material; it's that waxed, waterproof stuff that the wealthy get their jackets made out of. I'm not really comfortable because I don't fancy sharing the ditch with our furry friends of the countryside but there's no alternative. I suppose there's no chance of any sleep tonight, anyway.

Carl and I are feeling snug now and wondering what's happened to the others. We begin to talk about our favourite books and I just remember Carl telling me about an author called JP Donleavy, when I suddenly twitch and realise I'm nodding off to sleep.

I wake up to the morning light and the sound of the twittering birds. There's not a breath of wind. I look at my watch: 7:10.

The air smells beautifully fresh and luckily for us there's been no rain.

At 10 o'clock we enter the festival field. Those on the gate search everyone for contraband.

After surveying the area we plonk ourselves down at a reasonable distance from the stage. The roadies and workmen are doing the final electrical and mechanical safety checks. There's the occasional feedback from the microphones that make an unpleasant squeak that's enough to burst your eardrums but Carl and I are more interested in other things. We must find better ways to make our four-night stay in this rural part of Lincolnshire, as pleasant as possible.

Suddenly, we're jumped-on by our mates who've set-up both their tents not 25 yards away from us. I'm feeling envious of their rainproof accommodation, now.

We've brought our squares of canvas with us but neither of us is convinced they will be enough to protect us for the next three nights. We continue to look around for ideas, then we both spot some bales of straw in the neighbouring field.

Carl looks at me, then at the bales, then back at me.

"Yep. Whatever you're thinking, Carl, I agree" I say.

So, 10 of us spend the next half hour borrowing straw bales and constructing a magnificent two-berth home. It even has an entrance tunnel to lessen the draught.

Then Ged says, "I don't want to alarm you two but did you hear about those people at that festival last year?"

"Which people, what festival?"

"Those who built a shelter of straw at the Leeming Festival?" says Ged, darkly.

"Oh yes. I heard all about that ages ago" replies Carl, thinking Ged's just having a laugh. "Didn't a big bad wolf come and blow it all down?"

Everyone laughs, especially Rob Sheriff who nearly chokes on the fizzy pop he's swallowing.

"No, I'm deadly serious" says Ged. They all survived the fire but they were badly burnt."

I look at Carl's face and it's enough to stop a clock. Then I notice scores of people smoking. Our palace suddenly looks more like a death trap.

"If it was sunny and dry I'd be particularly worried. But everything's so damp I doubt whether petrol would set this shelter alight" I say, convincing no one.

Friday's stage acts are largely unknown so we spend our time watching the field fill up with festival-goers.

It's still damp and drizzly.

That night neither Carl nor I sleep soundly. I'm dreaming about various emergency scenarios. At about three in the morning I'm awoken by a loud noise. Carl is shouting and scrambling down the tunnel exit, kicking the straw bale out of the way in order to escape. It scares me witless but it's just a nightmare. We eventually get back to sleep, but this time I dream I'm trying to escape a fire and I can't locate the exit. I wake up with terrible claustrophobia.

Something has to change.

The straw is still damp but my plan is to make it permanently incombustible. So Rob, Derek, Steve, Ralph and Ged, help us to carry ten buckets of water to douse-down all sides of our temporary home. The walls are 18 inches thick and therefore, too dense for the water to percolate through to the inside. I'm confident it'll do the job intended and we'll sleep well tonight.

There are no washing facilities at the festival so by Saturday we're all feeling grubby and itchy. No one seems to be in charge of looking after the portable loos, either, so from Saturday lunchtime onwards they're all unusable. Most are unflushable and disgusting. Thank goodness we made our shelter well away from them.

Saturday's bands and soloists are outstanding. I've always loved Rod Stewart's, *Maggie May* and *Reason to Believe* and the hairs on the back of my neck stand up when I hear them sung live.

On Sunday we awake to the same cold, damp weather but at least Carl and I slept much better, and later in the morning we meet a couple of nice girls from Leeds while we get served at the burger bar. At the time I wasn't very good at chatting up lasses so I don't even try, but Carl's ultra confident. We each buy a giant hotdog and smother them with boiled onions and sauce.

The smart lass in the queue with dark hair says,

"Wow! You've got a big one!"

I smile pathetically but Carl doesn't.

He looks at the girls, then the hotdog, then back at the girls and says,

"Thank you. That's the best compliment I've had all weekend." And both young women guffaw loudly.

The ice is broken and we spend the final 24 hours in their company. They're both attractive and educated – a bit out of our league, actually. I mention this to Carl.

"Ey up, Carlos" I whisper. "These lasses are not just bonny, they're student teachers an' all."

"I know" says Carl "But don't let that put you off. No one's perfect. Be thankful for small mercies and stop complaining."

"Oh no, I'm not complaining" I try to tell him, but he and the little blonde student, Valerie, have now set off to get closer to the stage. Carl wants a better view of the Beach Boys.

Laura and Valerie head off back to Leeds early Monday morning and it's a great pity because they miss Don McLean's rendition of *American Pie*, which is only eclipsed by his, *Starry Night*.

The Great Western Pop Festival at Bardney is an experience I'll remember forever but it does feel heavenly to get back home again. Now I can soak in a tin bath full of hot soapy water, dine on my mother's homemade meat and tatie pie and sleep in my own safe bed. Moreover, it feels like a luxury to use a sit-down loo for the first time since Thursday morning. I never thought I'd be so pleased to see a sparkling clean toilet, even if I do have to walk across the yard to reach it.

A couple of days later, Carl says:

"Mark my words, Ronnie Steele, one day you'll write all about our weekend at the Bardney Pop Festival. I just know you will."

And I smile because I know there's not a snowball's chance in hell of that ever happening.

(This tale is written as a tribute to my great friend, Carl Ashton, 1950 – 1987. Still badly missed.)

BARNSLEY 'TIN 'OYLE'

It's 1973 and the people of South Yorkshire have good reason to be extremely proud of the Barnsley Canister Company. The factory stands on a steep hillside, near the police station, right in the heart of town and is known as "the greatest tin factory in the world". Its products are so well-designed and constructed, they dominate the domestic and international markets and their distinctive tea caddies and biscuit barrels, in particular, can be seen in almost every home in the country.

Many of these fine tins are later re-cycled for storing sundry items such as small change, screws, nails, batteries etc.

However, despite the civic pride felt for the company's international success, the respect it gets from Barnsley folk is undermined by the desperately low pay and dangerous conditions of its workforce – mainly females. Its staff turnover is deplorable and its record of workplace injuries is shocking.

To make things worse there's a definite element of social snobbery related to the firm, which leads to the Company becoming the object of ridicule. Most locals give it the unflattering nickname, the Tin 'Oyle, and when people hear of its official name it's usually greeted with a chuckle, followed by:

"Barnsley Canister Company? Wow! That sounds really grand... but don't you mean the Tin Oyle?"

And it's commonplace for even fathers to warn their daughters that unless they work hard at school, they might suffer the ignominy of being employed there.

In the spring of 1973, Mavis Jackson starts work there because her husband's in a low paid job. However, what mainly attracts her to the post is that the Canister Company organises shifts to suit young mums. Shifts start for some, just after children are dropped off at school and end in time for mums to pick up their kids as school finishes. That's ideal for Mavis because she has two young children.

Mavis quite enjoys her first week on the job. Employed in the "Fancy Box" department, her job is to clean the insides of tins, so they become completely grease-free. These include Strepsil and Henry Winterman cigar tins. To add a little variety to the job, she also screws knobs on to biscuit tin lids. Mavis suffers a couple of very minor cuts to her hands and the work is repetitive but the fun she experiences from the witty banter of her workmates, easily outweighs the negatives. The women love exchanging tales of life in their neighbourhood and the daily experience of recounting stories has turned many into accomplished raconteurs. Moreover, Mavis makes several good friends, and collects a much-needed, albeit fairly light, pay-packet at the end of the week.

After her Friday shift, she walks past the Town Hall towards the bus station, with her new workmate, Elsie Jubb. As they head down Regent Street, Elsie takes a new biscuit tin out of her shopping bag.

"What's that? Asks Mavis as they pass the opticians.

"Perk of the job" says Elsie, looking pleased with herself. "In lieu of unpaid wages."

"Won't you get reported to the police if you're caught?" says Mavis.

"No. They never check and if you do get rumbled you'll only get a written warning because they're desperate for workers" she says, stubbing out her cigarette with her thumb and first finger.

"Ooh, it really is a lovely biscuit tin" says Mavis "but I'd be terrified of getting 'done'. I've never stolen anything in my life."

"Oh, they're all at it" replies Elsie. "They say the boss's house is festooned with tins of every kind and I doubt he pays for 'em."

"Who told you that?"

"One of the lasses in the Despatch Department has a friend whose cousin cleans for him and his wife" answers Elsie.

As the weeks pass, Mavis gains experience in various departments in the factory but it's all boring work. However, one day she's reminded of the dangers facing employees on the factory floor.

Elsie has been asked to work in the Cutting department, which demands more skill but is more deadly. Her machine keeps jamming because a few pesky pieces of tin continue to get in the way. So, she removes her right safety-glove but forgets to replace it when picking up a long thin piece of metal with her right hand. The wafer-thin tin bites deep into the heel of her hand like a razor and blood gushes out.

The alarm goes up and everyone in the Cutting Department is so concerned, production stops.

Then over the tannoy a man's anxious voice can be heard:

"Could Mrs Jackson come to the office immediately, please? That's Mrs Jackson to the office please, immediately."

Mavis drops everything, and wonders what the emergency might be. Is it inside the factory or has something happened to her kids?

"It's Elsie Jubb" says Mr Garside, the manager, looking as white as a sheet. "She's broken the safety regulations and caused herself a bad wound."

"Oh, thank you, God" says Mavis, feeling relieved.

"W-W-What? Stammers Mr Garside. "What did you say?"

"Oh, I'm sorry, Mr Garside. I'm just so relieved that my kids are all right. I was starting to panic that something might have happened to them."

"Oh, I see. Erm yes, I mean no, nothing's happened to them. I'm sure they're fine. It's your friend, Elsie Jubb who's suffered an accident. Would you be so kind as to go with her in the ambulance to Beckett's A&E? We'll pay you for the rest of the day" says Mr Garside, handing Mavis, Elsie's coat, handbag and shopping bag.

When Mavis reaches the Cutting Department, the machines are still shutdown. Elsie is sat on a backless stool with her bandaged hand pointing to the ceiling like a child in school eager to answer a question.

"Keep your hand held high" says the handsome factory first-aider, nicknamed Dr Kildare. "It'll stop the bleeding from your wound. It's not much more than a scratch but you'll need to go to hospital."

"Go to hospital? shouts Elsie, shaking. "I'll need to change my knickers first."

"Change your knickers?"

"Yeah, I've just gone and peed missen" replies Elsie. And water can be seen dribbling down the front two legs of the stool.

At this sight, one of Elsie's colleagues retches and another feels faint.

In A&E, Elsie is taken into a cubicle and skilfully transferred from the stretcher onto a bed, by the ambulance workers.

Meanwhile, Mavis is told to go and sit in the waiting room but as she opens the curtains to go, she over-hears a nurse and a doctor.

"Suspected fracture and a possible heart attack in One and Two, and in Bay Three we have another casualty from the slaughterhouse."

Mavis looks at the sign above the cubicle she's just emerged from and reads it aloud, "Bay Three".

An hour and a half later, Elsie leaves the A&E Department with fifteen stitches and wearing what looks like a white boxing glove on her right hand.

As they're waiting for Elsie's prescription to be made up, Mavis mentions the 'slaughterhouse' reference made earlier.

"Oh, it's only the medics having a little joke" says Elsie. "The doctors and nurses have called it that for years. They frequently have to deal with injured workers from the Tin 'Oyle" she adds, holding up her right hand, smiling. "Calling it the slaughterhouse is dead funny, anyway."

"Now go and ring for two taxis" instructs Elsie. "You need to go and pick your bairns up from school and I'll have to go and get Stan's tea ready. I'm quite looking forward to a fortnight on the compo.

Mavis continues working at the Tin 'Oyle for another two years but whenever anyone asks her about her place of employment she always puts on her poshest accent and says:

"Actually, I work at the Barnsley Canister Company, you know. You may have heard it by its other name: the Tin Hole." And everyone laughs at her pretentiousness.

When Mavis finally resigns to do a three year teacher-training course, her colleagues on the shop floor buy her an expensive pen as a leaving gift.

15 months after leaving, Mavis bumps into Elsie in town.

"Hiya, Elsie. What are you doing shopping at this time?"

Elsie replies: "What am I doing shopping? They only went and sacked me and nine others" she says, drawing on a cigarette.

"Sacked? You're joking!"

"No joke. Somebody bubbled us one Friday. The bosses searched everyone's bag at the end of the shift and we were all caught 'carrying'. Meant the immediate sack for every one of us."

"Really?"

"Yep. Really" repeats Elsie, nodding her head. "But we're not bothered, lass. Five of us walked straight into better paid jobs at Slazengers and me and two others are studying for an Open University degree.

"Every cloud, hey Elsie?" says Mavis. "Listen, it's been lovely seeing you again but I've got to dash for the Wilthorpe bus.

"Have you to pick up the kids from school?" asks Elsie.

"Oh no. I want to get back home before the police raid the Wilthorpe branch of the Tin Oyle" says Mavis, joking.

And as Mavis rounds Burton's Corner to make her way on Eldon Street, she can still hear Elsie chuckling loudly to herself in the distance.

WHEN A PRICELESS EXHIBIT IS LOST FOR EVER

There's only one thing more embarrassing than losing a treasured possession and that's losing someone else's.

A unique pair of boots, on display at Cawthorne Museum, were once worn by Tom Parkin, the 12 year old son of a local farmer. Tom was struck by lightning at home in 1930. He recovered to tell the tale but his boots were ruined and the story would have stayed parochial, had it not been for a writer who published a charming description of the museum and the boots. The article was later used by the GCE Examining Board to test teenagers in O Level English Language, and so the boots became famous, both far and wide.

After this nationwide exposure, the museum not only becomes a proud jewel in the Cawthorne crown, its exhibits are also borrowed by local schools to inspire creativity.

> *   *   *   *   *   *   *   *   *

In January 1978 I take up my first post as a teacher at Kexborough Junior, which is the neighbouring village to Cawthorne. I'm very fortunate to join a friendly and talented staff and we become like one big, happy family.

As a novice teacher, I'm not monitored and harassed, but all the other members of staff are happy for me to approach them to discuss any problems. I often wonder at the superb creative work the students of other teachers are achieving and occasionally I persuade different members of staff to demonstrate a lesson.

One day I'm standing in the corridor reading the creative writing of a class of eight year olds. I can see immediately that the standard is far higher than that of my own class. I wish I could inspire my nine and ten year olds to write like this.

Elaine Padgett is just emerging from her classroom when she sees me reading her pupils' work on the display board.

"Would you mind telling me how you get your kids to write so expressively?" I ask. "I'd love it if my pupils could match that."

"Not difficult, Ronnie" she says, as she searches her handbag for her diary. "Tell you what I'll do, I'll ask Peter Binns [head teacher] to take my class for half an hour and I'll pop in and do a demo lesson for you. Tomorrow, after morning break, okay?"

"Perfect" I reply.

Next day, Elaine enters my classroom carrying a cardboard box containing one of the historic Tom Parkin boots. The museum, very wisely, only loan-out one boot at a time. I sit at the back of the room with my pen and notepad at the ready as Elaine prepares to work her magic. I've already followed her preparatory instructions - to put all the children's tables together into a large square, surrounded by chairs.

She begins to ask questions in order to draw the children's attention to various things. Then she asks deeper, more imaginative ones like, what do you think caused this damage? How was it burnt? Who would have worn these? What happened to the person wearing them? If the boot was a person, what would it be thinking? Doing?

Elaine makes it look easy, like when you watch a professional snooker player make a hundred break and you say to yourself: Doesn't seem that difficult to me. After 15 minutes of clever questioning, discussion, and writing key words on the blackboard, she sets the kids off writing.

As I expect, the results are stunning. Claire Jukes, in particular, writes a very thoughtful piece in which she imagines she is the boot and has been captured, locked up and has to escape. I'm so impressed I show Claire's work to Phil Johnson who teaches another third year class and he agrees with my judgement.

Next day I tell my students the real history of the boot and that it's actually one of a pair. Their faces are a picture.

The following week I bring a stuffed kestrel into the classroom, which we've also borrowed from the museum, and go through the same procedure that Elaine demonstrated. It works a treat and I'm delighted with the end results.

The kestrel and boot eventually do the rounds and before long the whole school is filled with wonderful, creative work.

In the staffroom, one lunchtime, Barbara Bissett tells me she plans to use the boot with her class. So I deliver it the way I received it: wrapped in newspaper like fish and chips, placed inside a cardboard box.

I then forget all about it for the duration of the Easter holiday.

When we return to school however, there's mounting anxiety amongst the staff when it's noticed that the boot is missing.

Peter Binns is ashen-faced as he enters my classroom just before the 9 o'clock bell.

"You haven't seen the museum boot have you Ronnie?"

"Museum boot? No, I passed it on to Barbara before the holiday" I say, looking round at all the shelves as I speak, just to double check.

"Oh dear, oh dear" he says and dashes out of my room and up the corridor.

"Why? What's wrong?" I shout, but Peter Binns either doesn't hear me or hasn't got time to explain.

I nip into the staffroom to find out what all the fuss is about.

"It's the boot" says Judith. "It's mysteriously vanished. Looks like it's gone walkabouts."

"No mystery at all" jokes Phil Johnson. "That thing's spooky, I tell you. It's absconded, just as in Claire's story."

The deputy head, Pauline Beecroft, drives down to the school cleaner's house, about 300 metres away. When she arrives she bangs firmly on Mrs Hamby's door because she can hear the washing machine is on.

"Mrs Hamby. We can't seem to find a special exhibit that we borrowed from Cawthorne Museum. Do you remember seeing or moving it? It's a very old boot."

"Erm, no, love. I'm sure I'd remember seeing an old boot in t'classroom" she replies, tapping her bottom lip with her first finger and thinking hard. "Where wor it left?"

"Mr Steele put it in Mrs Bissett's room, wrapped in newspaper, inside a cardboard box!"

Mrs Hamby draws in her breath quickly. "In newspaper? In a cardboard box? Oh no! I thought it was rubbish - I did, honestly. So I put it in t'bin early this morning."

"Oh, thank goodness" says Pauline feeling mightily relieved. "We thought we'd lost the blooming thing forever."

"You probably have. Bin men have already been. They come at just after eight every Monday."

Without saying another word, Pauline jumps into her car and drives back to school.

Operation Boot Recovery, kicks into action.

Peter Binns orders me and Phil to check the large plastic bins outside while the rest of the teachers take all the children into the hall for registration. Meanwhile he and his deputy drive around Kexborough council estate like a pair of rally drivers, trying to locate the bin wagon. Pauline enters the estate

121

to the west of Ballfield Lane and Peter searches the many streets to the east. He keeps braking sharply and asking people, walking the pavement, if they've seen the bin wagon.

"Aye. Bin men came on 'ere abart an hour ago, love" says an old lady hobbling to the shops. "I should think it'll be at t'tip by now, though. Why, what yer lost?"

"A boot" shouts Peter Binns as he pulls away from the kerb."

"A boot? One boot? Is that all!" she shouts after the car. "Did it belong to a one legged man?"

Peter drives like a maniac to the tip and when he arrives he spots Pauline's green Capri already there.

"It's gone" she tells Peter. "The boot's gone. A wagon dumped its load half an hour ago and it was immediately ploughed into the earth."

Pauline watches as Peter approaches a foreman wearing a black and orange donkey jacket. She sees the workman shaking his head and Peter walking away with his head bowed.

Back in school, a fourth year girl takes a note round informing teachers that there'll be a staff meeting at lunchtime.

The atmosphere at the meeting is sombre.

"I haven't a clue what I'm going to say to the curator at the museum" says the head as he opens the meeting.

There's a long silence.

"Can't we buy another identical one to replace it?" asks Ivan Shaw, a fourth year teacher.

"My granddad never throws his old boots away. He'll be sure to have a good match" I say, trying to lighten the mood. And soon all the frowns turn to smiles.

But Pauline Beecroft doesn't see the funny side.

"Yes" she says, ironically "I'm sure no one will notice the bloody difference between a 1960s steel-toe-capper and one that a farmer's lad wore in 1930."

"I've got some old high heels, if they'll help. Would the museum visitors notice the difference?" says Hilary, and now even Pauline can't suppress a grin.

"Hmmm" says Ivan Shaw, looking serious for the first time in his life. "What if we buy a pair of really old boots, slash and burn them so they look like the genuine article, and get the museum to pass them off as the originals? No one will ever know."

Peter Binns is not impressed and lets out a deep sigh. "This is no good, so I want you all to keep this dark because if the press does get wind of it, it could prove very embarrassing."

The next day we all wait anxiously for the head teacher's return from a meeting with the museum's curator.

"All's well that ends well" announces the head, to our relief. "The curator was very understanding and says she'll work out a way of making everything right."

Consequently, we forget about the boot and although we feel guilty for losing it, we do gain solace knowing that our gaffe has been kept secret. However, we're made to sweat a bit when The Sun newspaper prints half a tale.

One day someone anonymously leaves a copy of the rag on a coffee table, in the staffroom, opened at a particular page.

I see there's a very short piece with the headline:

"HISTORIC BOOT LOST

A historic boot, loaned from a museum in Cawthorne, Barnsley, was lost when a school cleaner mistook it for garbage and threw it in the bin. The lost exhibit once belonged to Tom Parkin, the 12 year old son of a farm worker, whose boots were struck by lightning. Fortunately, Tom survived the ordeal.

A spokesman for Mexborough Junior School denied any knowledge of the missing boot."

Luckily for us, shabby journalism means The Sun gets the most important fact completely wrong. By confusing Kexborough with the nearby town of Mexborough, we're let off the hook and our blushes are spared.

In the late spring of 2022 I visit the museum for the first time since our embarrassing blunder and fess-up to the voluntary curators. Fortunately, he and his wife see the funny side to the story and are pleased that the mystery of the missing boot is at last fully explained.

THE PRICELESS EXHIBIT

THE MINERS MARCH BACK TO WORK

It's March 1985 and the year-long miners' strike ends in defeat for the workers. Today, hundreds of Barrow Colliery miners are proudly marching back to their pit, behind their brass band, the union banner and Arthur Scargill their national leader.

The route of the march takes them past Corah's clothing factory in Worsbrough Bridge.

Corah's make high-quality clothing for Marks and Spencer and employ many female workers from the Barnsley area. Most of the machinists have male relatives who work at Barrow.

During the strike a few of them have been active in the Women Against Pit Closures movement that organises the soup kitchens for the miners and their families. A few even go picketing in the Nottinghamshire area.

The senior management at Corah's, which is largely male, is particularly hostile to the strike and make it almost impossible for supporters to organise collections to help the miners' cause. Pro strike notices are torn from the union notice board.

Faye Litherland is an 18 year old machinist and shop steward for the Hosiery and Knit Workers' Union. She's happy to take on the role of union representative because the pay is pitifully low and the conditions are poor.

The factory floor is a vast area that contains hundreds of sewing machines, all organised in lines. Each row has a manager whose job it is to sort out minor production glitches and maintain discipline. Right in the middle of the factory is a large glass-walled office from which every corner of the factory can be surveyed by senior managers. It reminds Faye of the Nazi prisoner of war camps. Workers are forbidden from talking to each other during their shift and to reinforce this, blaring music is played to drown out conversation. Women who transgress are given a warning or have their wages docked, and if petty rule-breaking persists, they're sacked.

This morning the shop stewards arrive early and hold an impromptu meeting outside the factory gates.

Mavis looks stressed as she begins to speak. She takes a couple of draws on her roll-up and says,

"As you all know, me, my husband and kids have had it tough – like many other families - for the last 12 months, because of the strike. When my fella and his workmates march past here today on their way back to Barrow I'm coming out of work to cheer them on. If I'm the only one in the factory to do this, I'm still walking out, even if it means the sack. Nevertheless, I'm still hoping as many of you as possible will also walk out with me, in solidarity, for 15 minutes. It's up to you."

"But what if they sack us all?" says Jean, folding her arms defensively.

"They'll not dare, if we *all* come out? replies Janet. "They'll not want a strike at the moment with us having a full order book. They'll be shooting themselves in the foot if they provoke us, and they know it."

"I'm not so sure" says Doreen. I lost a day's pay last month for talking during the shift. Union did nowt for me. I can't afford to lose another."

"Ah, the union didn't help because you defaulted on your subs and you'd no excuse because *your* husband's not been on strike."

Hilda, who's the oldest of the shop stewards and well respected, has heard enough.

"For Christ's sake!" she shouts. "I wonder what some of you people have got running through your veins? Mavis and thousands of others have spent a whole year standing up for every miner in the country. So there's no way I'm gonna let her down. I'm walking out in solidarity no matter what the rest of you bloody well do."

"Hear! Hear!" shouts Faye. "I'm definitely with you. To hell with management and their threats. They treat us like school kids because we bloody well let 'em."

That final contribution from Faye helps tip the balance. In a quick show of hands, the women vote unanimously to abandon their work stations for 15 minutes between 10:55 and 11:10 that morning.

As they saunter into work, Mavis confides in Faye:

"We've had a year of soup kitchens and beans on toast at home but I'll tell you what, Kay. It's been the best 12 months of my life and I'd do it again."

Now they're at their machines, they have to spread the word round the whole factory. It'll not be easy but the women have developed ingenious ways of circulating a message. The upbeat music blasting out is designed as much to stifle conversation as it is to speed-up production. If a machinist turns her head to talk, it's spotted by the Line Manager or someone in the 'watch-tower', and nipped in the bud. To circumvent this, the lasses pretend they're singing along to the music but instead of uttering the usual lyrics, they make up their own.

At 10 past eight, the introduction to *Maggie May* can be heard over the tannoy and as Rod Stewart sings, Faye seizes her opportunity. Instead of singing "Wake up Maggie I think I've got something to say to you" Faye sings:

"We're walking out before 11, will you all join us?

We're walking out before 11, will you all join us?

We're walking out before 11, we're walking out before 11

We're walking out before 11, will you all join us?

Angie, who works immediately in front of Faye, takes up the new lyrics and is bellowing them out to Dawn in front of her, and before the end of the song, three lines of machinists are joining in.

Their line manager, Miss Pinnock, has worked here for years. Some say her partial deafness has been brought on by the incessant noise from the machines. However, her disability has made her particularly adept at reading lips, so she tries her best to decipher the secret message.

"Dawn, Dawn, what are you singing?" she shouts.

"It's just the words to Maggie May, Miss Pillock."

"What? I can't hear you. Look straight at me when you speak" demands Miss Pinnock.

This time Dawn does turn her head slightly so she's looking directly at Miss Pinnock.

"It's-the-lyrics-to-Maggie-May-Miss-Pillock" she shouts slowly, as though she's addressing an imbecile, and it makes her colleagues titter.

Fortunately, Miss Pinnock can't distinguish between the words 'Pinnock' and 'Pillock' when lip-reading.

"What are you all laughing at?" she screams. "Shut up! Shut up! Stop laughing or I'll report you!" But this makes them laugh even more,

Then Miss Pinnock starts mumbling under her breath: "Oh, you're nowt but scum. All of you. But I know what you're up to. You'll not fool me."

The workers watch her walk through the door into the 'watchtower' bowing and scraping and telling the tale to senior management.

Those behind the glass walls now begin to monitor each area more closely. Nonetheless, all they see are women doing what they always do – getting on with their work and singing along to the songs.

One track later, the music stops and the assistant manager speaks down the microphone.

"Ding dong!"

"Avon calling!" chorus the machinists in unison.

"Ladies on the shop floor: It's been brought to our attention that some of you are planning to leave your machines at just before 11 to cheer on the miners as they march back to work.

"If that is what you're contemplating, think again because any worker who attempts this will be dealt with severely by management. For the rest of the day all cigarette breaks are cancelled. Thank you."

This creates a loud groan from the shop floor but at least the tannoy message has conveyed their secret plans to all the workers.

Before the loud music is switched back on by management, Dawn says, "Come on Faye. Carry on where you left off. I was enjoying that singing. They can't do us for singing, can they?"

From then on, Faye becomes the conductor of the choir. When *Radio Gaga* is played she quickly alters the words to fit the subversive scheme.

Freddie Mercury's voice is drowned out in the chorus as Faye can be heard singing,

"All we hear is, out for 11

Out for 11

Out for 11"

And at the end of each line the women bang down on their table twice just as in the song.

Soon the whole factory is joining in and Corah's PLC sounds more like the Ponte End at Oakwell after the Reds have scored the winning goal.

Those in the 'watchtower' are getting increasingly worried that they're losing control. The general manager's voice can actually be heard because the microphone has been unintentionally left on. He suddenly turns on his deputy who made the first announcement:

"Well that was a bright idea, wasn't it? I just knew this would happen if you stopped the cigarette break" he bellows. "Have you never heard the phrase, 'stirring up a hornets' nest'? Sometimes I think you have the brains of a flaming gnat!"

The women can't believe what they're hearing and there's much mirth.

The cigarette breaks are hurriedly reinstated but the warning of serious consequences for those who walk out is repeated over and over again.

At precisely five minutes to 11, Kay and the other shop stewards switch off their machines, push back their chairs and stand up. How many will join them? They don't know. Faye can feel her heart thumping inside her ribs.

Suddenly everyone else in her section also stops work and stands up, followed by workers in every part of the factory. They move like a flock of starlings, towards the exit door, with the line managers rooted to the spot.

Those in the 'watchtower' look on, powerless.

It's at this stage that all the women experience a thrilling sense of their collective power - especially now the music's been turned off and the din from the street can be heard. For the 18 year old Faye, it's the first time in her life that she's experienced such exhilaration at work and it feels magnificent.

Outside, as far as the eye can see, both pavements are lined with people, waving homemade banners, chanting and blowing whistles.

Faye starts to read the messages, crudely painted on scraps of cardboard:

"EVERY DOG HAS ITS DAY"

"PROUD OF YOU DAD"

"WE SHALL OVERCOME"

"BETTER TO FIGHT AND LOSE THAN NEVER FIGHT AT ALL"

"LOVE YOU GRANDDAD"

"F**K THE TORIES"

At the far side of the road is a woman dressed in a white smock and hat, holding a blue megaphone, shouting continuously.

MEGAPHONE WOMAN: What do we want?

CROWD: Thatcher out!

MEGAPHOME WOMAN: When do we want it?

CROWD: Now!

200 yards up the road their heroes are approaching. The brass band, playing the *William Tell Overture,* gets louder with every step. Some of the machinists are on the pavement but many are standing on the low perimeter wall, cheering and clapping.

Almost everyone is weeping as the march reaches the factory gates; but they're tears of immense pride.

Then the brass band has a rest and only the big drum can be heard beating to the step of the marchers.

Boom! boom! boom! boom!"

Suddenly a large group of women from the factory begin to sing:

"Here we go, here we go,

We're the women of the working class

We are women, we are strong

We are fighting for our lives..."

And the rest of the crowd join in with the song they've sung along to, so many times before.

As the marchers head towards the old level crossing, the cacophony subsides gradually and it's time for the women to return to the factory.

Most of the women are crying and Mavis in particular is sobbing so hard she has to be held up by colleagues.

As they re-enter the building, Miss Pinnock stands in the foyer with a face like thunder, She's been told not to say anything but she can't help herself.

"Losing pay for a bunch of communists. If I was prime minister I'd poison the lot of you." she sneers.

"Aye, and if you were prime minister we'd all happily take it" says Faye, bristling with anger.

AFTERWORD

None of the workers are ever called in to the 'watchtower' for censure and when they check their wage packets, not a single penny has been cut from their pay.

For the first time in her life, Faye has tasted the power of working class solidarity action and it's something she'll never forget.

Three years later, the Corah's factory in Worsbrough is shut down without so much as a whimper.

Now, Miss Pinnock is on the scrapheap herself, and has to suffer the ignominy of signing on the dole - like those so-called 'idle scroungers' she's detests. However, what's worse is, Miss Pinnock is not just without a job, money and dignity, she's also bereft of friends.

THE CHARM OFFENSIVE THAT FAILS

It's Monday 3rd March 1985 and I'm teaching at Keresforth Road Primary School, Dodworth, which is only half a mile from Dodworth Colliery.

Glen and Tracey approach me in class.

"Mr Steele. The miners' strike has finished today and our dads are marching back to Woolley Pit tomorrow. They'd like to know if we can have permission to march with them?"

I see all sorts of hazards in sanctioning this. First of all, I haven't the authority, but I also feel they'll be refused anyway if they ask the head teacher. Therefore, I simply tell them that if I was a miner I'd let my son or daughter miss school for one day and give the reason in a letter when they return. That way, permission can't be refused. If the authorities can sanction a day off school for a royal wedding, then a day off for this historic event can also be justified.

Then on Monday 18th March 1985, not quite two weeks after the end of the dispute, the South Yorkshire Police Service decides to launch a 'charm offensive' at our school. The aim is to restore the respect they've lost in mining communities.

All of our pupils and the ancillary staff, have close relatives who work in the mines. The adults in particular were all rock-solid behind the strikers but the teachers have stayed largely neutral in order to avoid big staffroom bust-ups.

Of the eight teachers employed here, I'm the only one whose father is on strike. However, one or two of the staff do make it clear to me that privately they detest Mrs Thatcher, the Prime Minister, but they haven't the confidence to openly support the miners.

The media deliberately complicates things by portraying the dispute as a clash between good and evil.

Thatcher versus Scargill:

Thatcher, the democratically elected 'hero' of the nation (according to those who own the media) versus the 'evil' Arthur Scargill, who has forced the reluctant miners to go out on strike against their will, for his own political ends.

The fact that the miners didn't trust the Tories and were willing to strike to save their jobs, is scoffed at by those who swallow Thatcher's lies.

After getting a drubbing at the hands of three of the anti-strike brigade, I decide it's better not to enter into arguments unless others raise the subject first. My colleagues are in the main, very decent people, but the continual demonisation of Scargill has brought the worst out in some of them.

Today, with very little notice, the police have decided to come into our school for a full week to try and restore the support they once had. It's a slimmed-down version of the old 'Police Fortnight' that used to be run in all Barnsley schools. It once included demonstrations of crowd-control by the use of police horses and dogs, but with the need to get their propaganda spread quickly, the use of these animals has been scrapped.

This week, instead of working with the whole school, the police try and convince only the older pupils that they're a force for good and deserve our support.

The deputy head, Phil Johnson and I, are both intensely annoyed by the nerve of the South Yorkshire Police to be trying this on so soon after the strike. However, we haven't the confidence or the union power to boycott it.

"It's just our two top classes that have been picked for this charm offensive, Phil. What a bloody cheek!" I say, as the children file into their respective classrooms.

"It's unbelievable" answers Phil. "It's put me in a foul mood."

"Me too. Most parents are going to be very annoyed and what are the kids going to think?" I add, as I leave the conversation to call the register.

Our head teacher, Don Ward, borrows several kids to set up the school library for the talk and slide show by Woman Police Constable Turton. After break time, all sixty-three of the top two classes are seated on chairs or tables at the hall-end of the library. The portable bookshelves have been wheeled to the sides and Phil and I sit on chairs on each flank of the students.

WPC Turton is quite an attractive young officer with a soft feminine voice – rather like someone you'd expect to front-up John Craven's Newsround or help little old ladies across the road. Listening to her dulcet tones makes it difficult to imagine her being anything other than a helpful friend.

The talk gets off to a good start. She shows slides of police officers in their uniform. She explains why a uniform and a tall, hard hat are very useful to bobbies.

"Now then" says the police woman "Who can tell me what dangers a police officer's tie, presents?"

A lot of hands shoot up with some straining to be picked.

WPC Turton points to Donna.

"Please Miss, a murderer might try to strangle you with your own tie" she answers, swinging her legs under the table she's sitting on.

"Oh, well done!" replies WPC Turton. "That's the perfect answer. Now, just to test your theory, would someone like to try and choke me with my own tie?"

This time even more hands reach for the sky, begging to be chosen. She picks Louise who rises from her chair at the front and walks over to the police woman.

WPC Turton says, "When I shout 'Go' I want you to grab my tie and pull me towards you like you're pulling a pony. Okay?"

Louise nods and her right hand is poised to grab the tie. There's a long pause. Everyone wonders how this is going to end.

The police officer looks at the audience and shouts,

"Goodness gracious me! it's warm in here" and turns away to open a window and everyone laughs at the anti climax. "Right, where were we?" she says, trying to recreate the mood.

"You've got to be quick, Louise" says the Officer. "Are you ready?

Louise nods again.

Are you really ready?"

Louise nods yet again.

"Go!" says the Officer and Louise grabs the tie and tries to pull WPC Turton towards her but the tie just becomes detached from the collar and Louise falls backwards.

It's a clip-on tie.

The audience laughs uproariously. No one expected that, except the police officer who now thinks she's well and truly won the students over – but her increasing confidence is premature.

The children settle down for the next slide. It's a simple diagram of a human being, drawn using a thick black line. Down the outside of each arm and leg is another thick red line.

"Right" says the officer. "This diagram shows the only areas that a constable may hit a person with a truncheon. These areas are marked in red. This is so important I'm going to say it again. The outside of the arms and legs are the only parts of the human body that police officers are allowed to strike using their truncheon.

There's a short silence. Then I hear a mumbling and fidgeting. Some of the pupils seem puzzled and then, after what seems an age, Glen raises his hand. He doesn't wait to be told to speak; instead, slowly and politely, he says:

"Excuse me WPC Turton. That's not right, that. I've seen coppers bashing pickets over the head with their truncheons."

"Glen's right, Miss" shouts Gary, his mate. "I saw it on the telly an' all. Coppers were just clubbing this picket on his head and blood was pouring down his face."

"I saw it an' all" shouts Tracey.

Then 63 children who'd all seen this on TV at sometime during the last twelve months are now in uproar and the police woman has well and truly lost control.

And I'm thinking, what on earth did she expect the children to do when faced with an obvious lie? Did she really think they'd deny what they've seen with their own eyes?

The police woman looks to me and the deputy head to restore order but neither of us has the will to get annoyed with the kids. We're both far too angry over the blatant propaganda she's trying to force-feed them.

"Okay! okay!" shouts WPC Turton, trying to restore the peace herself and failing. "There were mistakes on both sides - mistakes by the police and mistakes by the pickets – I'll admit that. However what's important now is that we all forget about the past and move on. Are you listening to me?"

But nobody is listening. The situation is hopelessly out of control and I'm pleased that the police officer has been called out for her undiluted bullshine. Our students have done their community proud.

The next day WPC Turton can't make it, so she sends her apologies. In fact she cancels the rest of the week and doesn't return to Keresforth Road

Primary School again. Perhaps she and her bosses realise that the whole concept of pretending the police's role was neutral during the dispute, just won't wash, at least for a generation.

AFTERWORD

A few years after the Great Strike, all those miners who put their trust in Thatcher and 'scabbed', find their 'safe' pit is to close and they're assigned to the scrapheap. Moreover, those union leaders who egged them on to undermine the cause, are nowhere to be seen.

Thatcher proved to be the liar, not Scargill.

The police's illegal role at Orgreave is highlighted in a Channel Four documentary in 2001. However, the rest of the media try to deny the accuracy of the evidence.

In 2012, a group that calls itself, The Orgreave Truth and Justice campaign, is formed to agitate for an enquiry.

10 years later, at the time of publishing, none of the leading political parties support an enquiry - citing feeble excuses.

It makes you wonder what they're afraid of.

Phil Johnson

SCHOOL TRIP TO FLAMBOROUGH

(Please note: Although this story is factually accurate, the names of people and places have been changed to avoid embarrassment)

I've spent three happy years teaching at Kerry Road Primary but in two day's time I'm heading for pastures new.

Today is Wednesday 24th July and everyone's excited. There are 33 in my top class including one child who's been absent through illness, plus 15 parents and grandparents who volunteer for a day at the coast. The idea is for them to fill up the 52 seater coach and make the cost per pupil more affordable.

At 8:30 am the children collect their packed lunches and get ready to board the coach when a surprising figure turns up. It's Darren. He's the one who's been absent for two full weeks so I assumed he wouldn't be turning up today.

"Ey up, Mester Steele, can I go on t'class trip?" he says wiping away the runner from his nose.

Oh, I just love this kid. Although I've taught him for two out of the last three years and he seems to have learnt very little, he's still my favourite. I know, I know... as a teacher you're not supposed to have favourites but I convince myself that I keep it well covered up.

"Darren" I say "You need three pounds for the cost of the trip... and you can't bring your dog."

"I've got three quid here Mr Steele" and before I can stop him he's pouring three pounds worth of warm change into my hands. "If our Patch can't come, Mester Steele, he'll walk home by his sen when t'bell goes."

I look from Darren to the dog and then to Darren again. They both look so sad.

"Alright" I say. "You can come but I'm sorry, not the dog."

"Yes! yes! yes!" he shouts in celebration. "I can go!"

"Oi" I say. "Before you start celebrating, I've to get written permission from your mum or dad and you need a packed lunch."

Unbelievably he produces a grubby reply slip signed by his mum and shows me his packed lunch in a blue carrier bag that he's collected from the table.

"That's someone else's packed lunch, Mister*. Look, I'll tell you what I'll do. I'll share *my* packed lunch with you. How's that grab you?" I ask.

"Spot on Mester Steele" he replies and now I know he's taking the Mickey because 'spot on' is a favourite expression of mine.

"Oh, and one other thing" I say. "Remember in June when we went to the Dam and you smuggled a field mouse into your pocket? I don't want any contraband on the coach today, Darren."

"I don't keep them contra-thingies, Mester Steele. I've only got two ferrets now. I'm trying to breed 'em. I want some baby ferrets but it's not working."

I take half my sandwiches, an Albert Hirst pork pie, an apple, a bag of crisps and a bottle of tap water, put them in a carrier bag and pass them to Darren.

"Can you carry it for me, Mester Steele?"

"Can I carry it for you? Do you want me to give you a piggy back onto the coach as well?" I say sarcastically.

"No, it's alreight, Mester Steele, I can walk" he smiles.

By 8:40 all the children and the fifteen adults are sitting on the coach in the school playground eager to depart. I'm last on, do a quick head-count of adults and students and then to the coach driver I shout "Wagons Roll!" and we're off. As we descend the steep drive towards Keresforth Road, a massive cheer goes up. I've undertaken many school trips but this is the first time I've heard such a celebration.

I sit next to Darren half way down the coach. He's bagged the window seat.

"Here, take your coat off, Mister" I say, "you're going to be red hot."

Darren slips off his thick hooded coat and I place it on the rack above my head.

"And your packed lunch? I might as well put that on the rack while I'm at it."

"I've eaten it, Mester Steele."

"What? You've eaten it! What are you going to have for lunch, now?"

"Oh, I'll just have my dinner, I think. I don't need my packed lunch as well."

Darren has no idea why most of the girls and boys around him are laughing their heads off.

The journey to Bridlington is fascinating. I'm so used to Darren hardly uttering a word that I'm surprised that he seems to be talking constantly. He wants to know what's this and what's that and why and where and who and how.

He points to a pylon.

"What's that?"

"A pylon"

"What's it there for?"

"To carry electricity to people's homes."

There's none of them pythons where I live."

"They're called pylons and you might not have seen any round your way because they can be dangerous."

"How come?"

"If you touch the wires you'll be fried to a blackened crisp, instantly."

"Ah ah. No one can reach that high" he says giggling. "only a giant."

"True, but if you fly a kite near the cables, the electricity can rundown the string and burn you alive."

"Really?"

"Why don't we see any pythons round our way?" he asks.

"They're buried in the ground."

"Why?"

"It's safer" I say.

"Why aren't they all buried in the ground then?"

"Excellent point, Darren, excellent point" I say.

By the time we reach Brid I'm exhausted but Darren's curiosity had been whetted and I come to the stunning realisation that he's never before been out of Barnsley until today.

The first hour in Brid goes really well. The children have been well prepared. They've already learnt about limestone and flint; lighthouses and shipwrecks; coastal caves and smugglers; the Viking invasions and defensive dykes. Therefore, what the children see today, is just designed to reinforce all these concepts.

We spend a good hour on the beach and then take the promenade train to the Sewerby Park area. From there we go to Dane's Dyke and then board a small boat to Thornwick Bay. Some of the adults don't fancy a boat ride on the North Sea so they stay on the coach, which will meet us at Flamborough.

After disembarking from the Saucy Sally we walk up the steep slope from the Bay to the car park where our coach awaits us. It's a very hard climb because the hot July sun has made us all so tired and thirsty.

"It's been a lovely day, Mr Steele" says one granddad in his 50s "Thank you. But this hill climb is damned killing me."

When we get near the top of the landing we can see a cafe in the distance with a Wall's Ice Cream sign outside.

Donna asks if she can buy one and as soon as I agree, she and all the others are off like lightning. Darren sticks by my side.

"I'm dead thirsty me, Mester Steele."

"Me too, Mister. Me too."

"I'd love an ice cream, me" he says.

"Hmmm... I could murder one myself" I reply.

Outside the cafe is a smaller sign saying "Ice cream cornets only 25p"

I feel two pound coins in my hip pocket.

"Listen Darren. Don't let on to the others that I'm treating you but here's a couple of quid. Get two large ice creams. I'm fairly certain it won't come to more than a pound, so don't forget where the change lives."

"Wow! I'll not Mester Steele" and he goes speeding off to the cafe shouting, "Mester Steele's not buying me an ice cream, honest he's not?"

Two minutes later he returns with two of the biggest cornets I've ever seen in my life. They are tri-cones with a generous dollop of vanilla ice cream in each compartment, strawberry juice, nuts and three flakes.

"Blood and sand, Darren. These are massive. Where's the change?" I say, holding out my hand.

"Oh, there was no change, Mester Steele. It shoulda come to £2.20 but woman's let me off wi' 20p" he says, licking the ice cream as it dribbles down the side of his cornet.

A minute goes by and I say: "Now tell me, Darren. What was your mam thinking of, sending you on a school trip with no pocket money?"

Darren stops licking and looks up at me quizzically.

"No pocket money? My mam gave me this" he says, pulling out a fiver from his pocket. "But I'm saving up to buy two baby ferrets."

AFTERWORD

Many years later I bump into Darren at a party and we have a shrewd political discussion. I also discover he's had great success as a sportsman, winning national titles and although he's still in his early thirties he's already become a successful business man.

And that's all I'm willing to say. I daren't give too much away because I really don't want readers to identify who was possibly the most interesting and likeable kid, I ever taught.

*I often addressed boys as 'Mister' and girls as 'Mrs', for good reasons:

1. It made them smile.

2. If I didn't know a child's name it was easier to get their attention by saying, "Hey, Mister (or Mrs)" rather than say "Hey, you with the red hair and green top. Yes you, in the middle of the back row..."

Flamborough

STRANGE BUT TRUE

The winter of 1987 is so cold it becomes known as The Big Freeze. The song, "The Final Countdown" by Europe, is still riding high in the charts in mid January.

Michael Bray is over from Australia for a three-week holiday. He left his wife, Barbara, and three children behind, enjoying the glorious Wollongong summer. Mike and Barbara take it in turns to visit England, because holidaying the UK, as a family, is too expensive.

Whenever they return to England they always make sure they visit each other's relatives, and on this particularly cold January day, Michael travels north from Barnsley to Leeds to visit his sister-in-law.

After a pleasant afternoon, Mary's husband, David, drives him back to Leeds City railway station but when Mike goes through to the entrance hall, he finds that all trains have been cancelled. The chalkboard message blames ice on the tracks and says a further bulletin will be issued at 21:30 hrs. David's already driven away, so to pass time Mike looks for a pub that appears warm and inviting.

It's Saturday evening and the pub he chooses is quite full and the atmosphere seems good. He buys a pint and stands at the bar looking rather cool in his Australian stockman's coat and akubra hat. A tall young man comes to the bar for refills.

"My goodness... I like your coat and hat mate" says he, taking a ten pound note out of his wallet.

Mike replies that he's brought them over from his home town of Wollongong near Sydney. Immediately, the man is fascinated and introduces himself as Jan Palowski and says he'd love to hear more about living in Australia as he's seriously considering emigrating there himself.

"I'm Michael Bray. My family love Australia and I definitely recommend it."

"Here Michael", says Jan, "Let me get you another pint and you can join our group and tell us all about Oz."

Mike is then introduced to Jan's wife, Pauline, and the other four friends and they spend almost half an hour discussing the many advantages of living on the other side of the world. Then Mike explains that he has to catch the 22.05 train back to Barnsley – if it's running. They all shake hands, as Mike leaves for the fifteen minute walk to the station. As he steps into the street he pulls his hat down tighter over his forehead to stop the biting wind from snatching it away, then crunches unsteadily over the ice-covered pavement. The arctic wind numbs his cheeks and ears and when he reaches the empty station he sees the chalkboard has indeed been updated.

"PUBLIC ANNOUNCEMENT

All British Rail services operating from Leeds City railway station have been cancelled until tomorrow (Sunday) midday, due to ice on the tracks.

We apologise for any inconvenience.

Station Manager"

Shit! Mike asks at the ticket office about the bus service to Barnsley and he's told those have also been cancelled for the rest of the evening. He checks his pockets again and finds his return rail ticket, a Mars wrapper and 35p covered in blue fluff. In his wallet is a fiver which is not enough to cover the taxi fare back to Barnsley and he's not brought his bank card with him. He starts to panic. What on earth should he do? He couldn't walk it home, it's too far and much too dangerous. Besides, he's read of people freezing to death in these conditions. Hmmm, what about going to the police station to see what they suggest? They'll probably just laugh. So Mike resolves to head back to the pub, where it's warm, in order to consider the alternatives.

God! Being stranded, miles from Barnsley, is a living nightmare.

Jan and his friends are still in the pub.

"Not a problem, mate" says Jan, making sure he gets the okay from his wife, Pauline. "We've got a spare room. You can stop at ours".

"What? Oh no" says Mike, taking another drink of his beer. "I really don't want to impose."

"Don't be daft. You're not imposing at all. You're staying at ours and let that be an end to it" interjects Pauline as another member of the group rises from his seat to buy a further round.

"I really can't believe this" says Mike. "You've all been so kind." He feels so blessed his eyes moisten as he hears the chorus to *The Final Countdown* over the music system and a big cheer from the lads at the nearby pool table as the winning black ball is sunk.

At eleven, the taxi arrives. It's only a short 15 minute ride to a nice end-terraced house where they live and it's only now that Mike starts to feel slightly uncomfortable. He doesn't really know anything about Jan and Pauline. They're strangers. In fact for all he knows, they could be crazed psychopaths who prey on lost individuals and kill them while they sleep.

Come on, Mike says to himself. Pull yourself together. These are very kind folk. Stop thinking like an idiot, for God's sake.

The spare bedroom and double bed are beautifully clean. Mike sleeps through the night like a baby until a chink of morning-light shows through a gap in the blackout curtains. It's almost 10 am, so he's slept much longer than usual. He looks out the back and over the fields and sees most of the ice has disappeared. It must have rained in the night. The sky is now a refreshing light blue and the world seems different, somehow. As he puts his trousers on to go to the loo he smells bacon and eggs frying downstairs.

"You know I'll need to pay you back for your hospitality" he says as he enters the dining room.

"No, don't be silly" says the Pauline. If you can't help a friend in need... "

"Oh stop it Michael" joins in Jan, smiling, as he hands Mike a large plate of breakfast. "Tell you what" he says mischievously, "You can either pay us £500 for bed and breakfast or you can accept that our kindness is absolutely free. Now what's it to be?"

"Okay then" says Mike, "You've twisted my arm."

"By the way" says Jan, "there'll be a bus on the far side of the road at ten past eleven, Michael. It'll drop you off just outside the railway station."

Soon after this, something weird happens. As he prepares to leave via the back door he notices a message-board on the kitchen wall, to the right of the back door. Pinned on it are a gas bill and phone bill, both with the name 'MICHAEL BRAY' clearly printed on them.

Whoa! Mike freezes like a statue, his mind racing. How the hell can that bill have my name on it? What the f**ks going on?

" Jan! Jan! What this? These bills have MY name on them: 'Michael Bray'. That's my name."

Jan doesn't bat an eyelid.

"Oh, don't worry about that. Michael Bray is also my adopted name" explains Jan. I came over from Poland as an orphan-child and my adopted-parents, the Bray family, gave me the name, Michael Bray. Just recently I've started to use my original name, Jan Palowski. That's all. Now come on and hurry up or you'll miss your bus".

"But why didn't you tell me that when I introduced myself last night? You showed not a flicker of surprise. And before I leave I want us to exchange names and addresses" says Mike, "so I can..."

"Go on, Mike" says Jan "Your bus will be here anytime."

Mike's in a state of shock but he feels that Jan is bundling him outside before he can find out anything else. He walks across the road and soon the 11.10 Metro Bus picks him up and rattles its way into Leeds.

When Mike reaches his sister's house in Monk Bretton, Barnsley, he tells the whole family all about the very odd events of the previous eighteen hours. His sister and nieces are all equally dumbfounded and what particularly troubles them is the laid-back attitude of Jan when Mike first introduced himself. They all know that Mike is not a fantasist and they're in no doubt that all the details are honest and accurate.

"You should have got his address" says Olive, his sister.

"I did try my best but I failed, and I could kick myself for it."

Next day, Michael is driven to Manchester Airport for the flight back to Sydney. Therefore, he never again gets the chance to revisit the Leeds pub in the hope of bumping into Jan and Pauline.

However, he's never in any doubt about what really happened that strange night in Leeds in 1987:

In his time of greatest need, someone or something was looking after him. And if you question him about it today, he'll insist:

"I know there's usually a logical explanation for weird incidents like this and retelling the story does expose me to ridicule, but I not the romancing type and I've never experienced anything like this before or since."

Uncle Mike and his sister Auntie Olive, with my dad in the middle.

AUTHOR'S VIEW:

My down-to-earth Uncle Michael's story is very strange. However, there are sure to be at least one or two fantastic coincidences in everyone's lifetime.

Perhaps this is the reason for such a freak occurrence.

(Published with the kind permission of my Uncle Michael)

THE COST OF DISCOVERING GENIUS

As a school teacher, I always feel that if you can combine fun and learning, you're onto a winner. That's why I love to play all sorts of intellectual games with my ten year old students. By employing such methods I've seen poor maths students suddenly blossom by playing a safe form of darts; and I've witnessed mediocre authors display their genius in creative writing.

One maths game I love to play, fairly regularly, is called the *Greater Than* game. It's brilliant for understanding fractions and probability, developing logic and learning the language of maths. I usually play it for 10 minutes between 3:20 and the end of the school day.

I always start off by telling my pupils that I'm thinking of a number between 1 and 100 and they have six guesses to get it. To make it easier for them they can ask "Is it greater than, say, 50?" - or whatever number they choose. If I say, yes, then they know the answer is between 50 and 100; if no, then it's between 1 and 50.

One day in the late 1980s I introduce the game to a smart class of 9 and 10 year-olds at St Hilda's Junior.

John Chivers is a bright lad so I pick him for the first game.

No one in the room knows that I've chosen number 5.

"Is it greater than 90, Mister Steele?" asks John, hoping the answer can be narrowed down to between 90 and 100.

John Chivers

"No, John, it's not" I reply.

"Megan smiles and whispers unhelpfully to John, "It's between 1 and 90, John."

"I know, I'm not daft."

Then John tries another guess: "Is it greater than 50?"

"Nope, it's not" I tell him. "Only four guesses left, John."

"Hmmm, is it greater than 10?"

"No" I say and suddenly there's a wave of excitement amongst the rest of the class. Some think they have it and are urging John to guess it. Helen has a hunch that it's 5 and says,

"John, John, it's 5, it's 5. I'm sure it's 5" as many others shout out different answers.

But John is not one to be rushed. He knows he has three guesses left and he's not going to waste any of them. He's now sussed out how to efficiently narrow the options down.

"Okay, Mister Steele. Is it greater than 5?"

"It is NOT, John" I tell him, and there's a loud "whooo!" from his classmates.

Two guesses left.

"Okay. Then it could be 1,2,3,4 or 5. Erm... in that case is it greater than 3?"

Yes, it is, John" I say "but you've only now got one last guess."

"Right. Then the number you are thinking of Mister Steele must be either 4 or 5. So I say, you're thinking of number 4!"

"Oh, bad luck, John. I was actually thinking of the number 5" I announce.

There's a look of disappointment on many faces but Natalie Saunders is puzzled and sticks her hand up.

"What is it Natalie?"

Natalie Pearey

"Oh, nothing Mister Steele, it doesn't matter" she replies shyly.

"Come on, Natalie, speak your mind."

"Well, I was thinking, how do we know for sure that you really had number 5 in your mind? You might have been thinking of number 4 all along and changed your mind at the last minute."

"Oh, I see. Fair point. Now let me get this straight. You think your teacher is a big cheat? Is that it, Natalie?"

And everyone in the class giggles, including Natalie.

So I reply with mock disgust: "How dare you call me a cheat, Madam?" and the laughter continues.

But Paul Scattergood has different ideas:

"But Natalie's right, Mr Steele. How *do* we know you weren't cheating?" he says, smiling broadly.

I put on my meanest look and raise both fists like a boxer.

"See these Scattergood?" I say. "Fastest fists in Barnsley, these. They could knock out Giant Haystack in just three punches."

Everyone's laughing now.

Paul Scattergood

There follows an excellent class discussion about whether people should be fully trusted in a game like this. However, Lee Holland puts an end to the debate when he raises his hand and says,

"Well, I'll be honest, Mr Steele, If I thought I could get away with it, then I think I might be tempted to cheat" and everyone seems to agree with that because Lee is the type of lad you can rely on. Then, before I dismiss the children I tell them that before we play the *Greater Than* game again, they must work out ways of making sure I can't possibly cheat.

A week later the children ask if we can play our new game for a second time. Paul Scattergood feels it would be fairer if I write down the number I'm thinking of before we start, and all agree.

"All right then, I can take a hint. You clearly don't trust your poor, honest teacher" I say, as I take out my handkerchief; but instead of dabbing away my crocodile tears, I surprise everyone by blowing my nose loudly.

This time I choose Paul to guess the number. He's as sharp as a needle.

"All right, big-mouth... I mean, Paul Scattergood. You can go next" I say, as I write down the number 71 on a piece of scrap paper and turn it over so no one can see it.

The rest of the class offer Paul much encouragement:

"Go on Paul. You can do it."

Lee Holland

"You watch. Paul'll guess it right."

"It's 21" whispers another voice.

Paul is influenced by the last comment.

"Is it 21?" asks Paul.

"Nope" I reply. "That's one guess wasted. Only 5 more left."

Now Paul says, "Is it greater than 50?"

"Yep, it is greater than 50. You have 4 guesses left, Paul.

"Is it greater than 75, Mr Steele?"

"No, it's not, Paul. Three guesses left, mate.

"Is it greater than 62?" says Paul, and I can tell for sure that he's fully twigged how to narrow the possible answers down.

"It certainly is Paul. Two guesses left."

"Is it greater than 69?" he asks.

"Yes it is, Paul. Last guess, matey.

"So, if it's greater than 69 but not greater than 75, then it must be 70, 71,72,73, 74 or 75. Hmmm."

All the others in the class think they know which number is the correct one and they're all whispering their hunches.

After a long pause, Paul says, "Mr Steele the number you're thinking of is... number 72!"

I put on a look of great surprise and make an audible gasp.

"Did you say 72?" I ask.

"Yes! yes!" shouts everyone.

"Nope. It's not 72, it's 71. Bad luck, Paul" I add, displaying a smug expression.

"Aw! Mr Steele!" says Natalie "you're just teasing us. Can we have a look at that piece of paper you wrote on?"

"Be my guest."

From then on we play the *Greater Than* game once a week and each time my students are improving. Soon three out of every four who try, are successful.

One Friday I decide to up the ante.

"Today, anyone who guesses correctly will receive a pound coin " I announce, as I fish in my pocket for some change. I haven't got any one-pound coins but I know that my colleague, Pete Bevis has, because he collects our tea money each week. So I send John with a fiver from my wallet.

"Now take this five pound note, John, and ask Mr Bevis very politely if he will change it for five one-pound coins" I say. "Now repeat back to me what you've got to do."

John says, "I've to take this five-pound note to Mr Bevis and ask him politely if he will change it into one-pound coins."

Then I stand up and point to the classroom door and say to him sternly:

"Now go! And do not fail me!"

And John's laughing so much he nearly forgets to take the money off me.

Next I pick Jonathan (not his real name) to play for a one pound reward because he struggles quite a bit in Mathematics. This has nothing to do with me being a skinflint, you understand, but everything to do with implementing the school inclusion policy. Honestly.

I write down the number 45 on a piece of scrap paper and put it face down on my desk. Jonathan's limited understanding of number soon becomes clear when he utters his first question:

"Is it greater than 90?"

Then he tries 80,70,60,50, until he has one guess left.

Most of the rest of the class have their heads in their hands. I ask him: "How many possible right answers are there now, Jonathan?"

"Are there 50 left, Mr Steele?" he replies, feeling unsure.

"That's right, well done, Jonathan. Come on then. What number am I thinking of?" I say, knowing full well he hasn't a prayer of getting it right.

As he thinks, Jonathan has that pained look on his face that tells me he's trying so hard it actually hurts. His face is scrunched up, with one eye shut and the other one looking up at the classroom ceiling above.

"Is it 45, Mister Steele?"

"What?" I say, much louder than I intended.

"Is it 45?" he repeats.

"Did you say 45, Jonathan?"

He nods.

"Here you are mate. Well done" I tell him and as I give him the one-pound reward, the rest of the class give him a massive cheer.

If that wasn't bad enough, the next contestant is even weaker at number than Jonathan. Nicky Ridley narrows the correct answer down to between 70 and

100 and still gets it spot on when he says '86'. That means I'm £2 down at the end of the day.

The following week I have a theory that the children can work out the number I'm scribing by watching the movement of my writing arm. As a consequence, I plonk my briefcase on my desk to obscure the children's view as I write the secret number. The children fail in the first two games so on the third and final one I take out a pound coin again.

Once again, I pick on one of the low achievers - Hannah - and despite all my precautions, she guesses correctly even though she has ten possible numbers to pick from. What's the likelihood of that happening? I just can't understand it. There's no way the students can cheat, yet as soon as I offer a financial reward they manage to get it bang on, even if the odds against are big. This phenomenon continues regularly for the rest of the year and the rest of my teaching career.

I later discover that the former Poet Laureate, Ted Hughes, had a similar experience teaching maths to under-achieving 15 year olds at a Doncaster comprehensive school*.

All I can conclude is that the incentive of money simply brings out the genius in the kids of Athersley and New Lodge.

*Ted Hughes describes this in his foreword for Sandy Brownhill's book, *It Doesn't Have to Rhyme*.

VICTIMISATION FAILS

It's 1991 and I'm teaching nine and ten year olds at St Hilda's Junior School. I'm also very active in my union: The National Union of teachers (NUT).

Things are tough. Teachers' pay is threatened and there's huge pressure from the Tory government for our council to make even more savings. At first there's no indication how more cuts can be made but then comes a thunderbolt from the blue: the amount of money spent by Barnsley for children with learning disabilities is to be reduced by 50%.

This causes genuine fury amongst teachers because the savings will certainly make teaching and learning much harder.

As editor of the Barnsley NUT's newsletter, Kernel, I publish an article criticising the Council for implementing the cuts and in particular, Mr Smithson, an LEA advisor, for suggesting ways to save half a million quid.

A week later our head teacher, Brian Hawkes, calls a meeting. Mr Smithson will be coming into our school to assess teaching standards. He'll be observing a lesson by all twelve classroom teachers starting after break this morning.

"Mr Smithson wants to observe you first, Ronnie" says Brian, as he tucks a sheaf of papers under his arm and heads to the hall for the school assembly. "And for what it's worth I'm not at all happy about this, but there's nothing I can do."

All my colleagues look in my direction. Their suspicions are also raised.

"What a coincidence" says my friend and colleague, Pete Bevis. "One minute the union sends Mr Smithson a shot across his bows, the next he's coming into school to find fault. Hmmm... interesting."

At the end of the first lesson, I tell my class to expect a visitor after playtime and he's coming to see how well they are learning. I start to feel a bit nervous and drink my coffee in my classroom and hand out the children's jotters.

Each week at this time we have a writing lesson where the children are given fifteen minutes to write as much as they can on any subject. It's a good class with a fair number of very creative children so I'm very confident about the success of the lesson. I call it a Writing Derby – it's a bit like a writing race and it's designed to encourage children to write as much as possible without having too many hang-ups about spelling and punctuation. All the children love it and there's always utter silence apart from the sound of pencils scratching on rough paper.

Mr Smithson enters the classroom without introducing himself to me or the students. He sits in the library corner and pulls out an exercise book from his briefcase and fountain pen from his jacket pocket and starts writing. I do find this terribly disconcerting but the children completely ignore him because they're all eager to get off to a flyer in this writing race.

"Don't you be starting yet" I say to Elizabeth who appears to be scribbling something down.

"I'm only writing my title, Mester Steele. I'm not going to count that at the end."

"She'll not, Mr Steele", says her best friend, Alex. "She does that every week."

"Right children" I say, making sure everyone's in a position to start. "You're under starters orders and you're off!"

Mr Smithson gets up from his seat and attempts to walk round the room, looking at the children's work. However, the kids are uncomfortable with his presence. He's distracting them so they cover their writing with their arms and look daggers at him as he tries to pry. Mr Smithson decides it's prudent to retire back into the library corner.

After thirteen minutes I tell the children they have two minutes to finish off and when that time is almost up I count down from ten then blow the whistle to signal the end.

The children sit back, stretch and sigh. They start to gossip quietly about the unique topic they've covered. The next task is to count the number of words and make a record of this. Then they compare their word-count with their previous efforts.

After that the kids are given a few minutes to edit their work. As they complete the first edit they put their hands on their heads to signal that they wish to share their efforts with the rest of the group. After about five minutes almost everybody is sitting with their hands on their heads.

So far, so good. I keep glancing over to Mr Smithson and I see him scribbling like mad on his paper but I'm not concerned because everything's gone like clockwork, and as we approach the climax to the lesson I'm feeling supremely confident that things will end well.

Normally I ask a cross section of children to read out their writing but today I feel I have to fend off a threat to my career by selecting only the 'gifted' writers to share their work.

Joanne Bennett is a natural, uninhibited author, so I decide to choose her first. She starts by standing up, clearing her throat and trying not to smile:

"WHEN I SMOKED MY FIRST CIGARETTE"

(I have a quick glance around the class and everyone's paying close attention. The title has immediately grabbed the interest of Mr Smithson. His mouth is wide open. The other children are equally shocked that Joanne dares to write about such a topic.)

"Last year I went to visit my Grammer and when I was there I had to use the upstair's toilet. On the floor, under the sink was a cig. Grandad must have dropped it, so I picked it up, meaning to take it to him but then I thought, no. I wouldn't mind trying to smoke it myself. It's got to taste better than it smells."

(All the class burst out laughing.)

"It was the first time I'd touched a cig with my fingers and so when I picked it up I couldn't believe how light it was. I expected it to be as heavy as a pencil. Then I sneaked the cigarette into my anorak pocket at the bottom of the stairs. Later, when I got back to my house I found a cig lighter in the drawer. That Saturday evening, I went with my two best friends round the back of the garages to smoke it. I rolled the little wheel and the flame lit the cigarette end. I sucked on it and breathed it in. Straight away my legs went wobbly and I felt so dizzy I could hardly stand up. My friend, Sally said, "You owt to see your face Joanne, it's drip white." I started to cough and bent over and threw up my tea all over the side of the garage and my shoe. Sally and Natalie decided they didn't want a go at smoking cos their mums say it gives you cancer.

"Well thanks for that. Why didn't you tell me before" I said, spitting onto the floor.

When I grow up I don't think I'll ever smoke.

The end."

As Joanne finishes reading her story most of the children are doubled-up with laughter and burst out in spontaneous applause. I sneak a look at Mr Smithson and he's abandoned his notes and is also reluctantly applauding.

Next, I pick on Jamie Tetley. He's one of the brightest kids I've ever taught so I know it's perfectly safe to invite him to read his work out.

"ITALIA 1990

I'll never forget the summer of 1990 when England reached the semi final of the football World Cup. The tournament was called 'Italia 90' and was watched by more people than any World Cup in history. I didn't miss one England game and I saw all the goals from every match.

England started badly but once Bobby Robson got his team sorted out, we were looking like we might become champions of the world."

(As Jamie pauses while he turns over the page of his jotter, I take another quick glance around the classroom. Everyone is on the edge of their seats)

"Paul Gascoyne was playing like a genius and David Platt was scoring great goals. Before I knew it we were preparing for the semi against Germany.

"I felt really nervous for the semi and when Gascoyne was booked I cried just like Gazza did and cried again when we were knocked out on penalties.

"But more than anything, what I'll never forget about the whole tournament was the beginning and ending of each TV broadcast when they played Pavarotti singing Nessum Dorma. It was so fantastic.

"I'll don't think I'll ever forget 'Italia 90' and how the theme song made me feel. And I can't wait for the next FIFA World Cup competition."

As Jamie finishes there's a long pause and suddenly the whole class break out into whooping and cheering. He has managed to express in this short piece, everything that the other children had felt themselves during the competition.

And as the noise subsides, Mr Smithson rises from his chair, puts his exercise book in his briefcase, his fountain pen in his breast pocket and slips out of the classroom almost unnoticed.

"Thank you so much, Joanne and Jamie for reading out your work" I say. "That was absolutely... not too bad." And my comment is met by a roar of laughter because everyone is aware that what they've heard today is something extraordinary.

I'm so proud of all my students and feel relieved that they've performed so brilliantly when it really mattered to me. I find myself smiling when I think that Mr Smithson must have left my classroom thinking everyone of my lessons goes as well as this. Well, it's not up to me to put him straight, is it?

During lunch break, our head teacher, Brian Hawkes, comes into the staffroom and announces that Mr Smithson has left school and has not said when he'll be returning. My colleague, Pat, makes a rosette as big as a saucer and hands it to me. On it it says:

"YOU CAN'T GET ME

I'M PART OF THE UNION!"

In fact, Mr Smithson is never seen inside our school again and so I conclude that his claim to be assessing all our teachers was a blatant lie. Therefore, we were right to suspect that his covert aim was to victimise me. But he failed miserably.

However, he does succeed in making cuts of 50% to the Special Needs budget and in consequence making the job of teaching much more difficult.

What some will do to get on in life!

How do they possibly sleep at night?

Jamie Tetley   Joanne Bennett

LIKE BLOCKS O' ICE

During the winter of 1995/96 there's a succession of cold snaps that make Barnsley shiver; and those who work at St Hilda's Junior School suffer more than most because of a faulty heating system.

On top of that, the Local Education Authority (LEA) shut down the heating in all schools at the weekend, to save money. Consequently, when the Sunday air temperature is below zero the Monday morning classrooms are well below the legal requirement.

After one very cold weekend, parts of the school don't reach the legal minimum until the following Wednesday afternoon.

Today is another freezing Monday and it's so cold that the staff and children have to wear their coats and hats during lessons.

I'm seriously concerned because my eight and nine year olds are looking pale, miserable and devoid of enthusiasm. I notice they are sitting hunched up in an effort to maintain body heat. So, every fifteen minutes I interrupt their Maths and get them to do some simple warm-up exercises.

"Okay. Time to stretch a bit" I say. "Who volunteers to lead the seven-step warm-up?

The seven-step warm-up is a set of seven gentle exercises that all the children are familiar with.

Lauren leads it, starting with warming up her neck muscles by moving her head in a circular fashion. She then focuses on her shoulders, arms, body and leg muscles. The other children copy her.

"Now I'm going to give you one minute to do this next exercise as many times as you can." I explain, and as I speak, I step on a child's chair then step down again as a demonstration.

"You can work with a partner - one does the step-ups while the other counts and records the number. Then you change over. Okay? It's not a competition but if anyone wants to turn it into one, that's fine by me" I tell them.

At playtime the head teacher, Brian Hawkes, lets children choose to stay either in the classroom or in the school hall where they can use some of the Games equipment. Four of the teaching assistants agree to monitor the pupils whilst the staff has an emergency staff meeting.

I kick off the discussion: "This is just not on" I say. "No one can teach or learn in these conditions." And there's a chorus of approval from my colleagues.

"All my neck muscles are tense and I have the beginnings of a migraine" says one of our supply teachers.

"There's a girl in my class who's not dressed properly and she's actually shivering" says Brenda. I think she's in the early stages of hypothermia.

"Personally, I don't think it's that cold" says Judy, hoping to get some support "but then again I don't feel the cold. And it doesn't seem to be bothering my pupils, either."

"Don't feel the cold?" says Joan. "My fingers and toes are bloody numb. They're like blocks o' ice"

"If you don't feel the cold, Judy, would you mind swapping classrooms with me?" asks Jean, sounding irritated. Jean's classroom is one of two that's the farthest away from the boiler room.

Judy doesn't answer but looks down to the floor.

"We're all in *loco parentis*" utters Mrs O'Brien, our most senior teacher, in her broad Cork accent. "I tink we have a duty to our charges and a duty to ourselves as trade unionists to make sure the school is kept warm."

Judy joins in the discussion again: "I believe we have to be very careful not to provoke the LEA here. They can dig their heels in if we upset them. Let's try and box clever."

Brian Hawkes hasn't said a word yet. He can see most people are angry so he's giving everyone a chance to let off steam. When there's a hiatus in the discussion he finally speaks in a calm and collected manner.

"Colleagues, you're pushing at an open door with me. No adult should be expected to teach and no child should be expected to learn in such low temperatures. That's why I've already been on to the LEA to explain our situation. They say these are exceptional conditions and many schools are in the same boat. However, they're sending a heating engineer round later today to examine the boiler and pumps."

"Oh, bravo!" says Judy who is also keen to stay on the right side of the head teacher as well as the LEA. "That's just what I was going to suggest".

Then Brian turns to me:

"Ronnie, as trade union representative, would you ensure the temperatures in each classroom are recorded twice a day so we can present accurate data to the LEA" he says, as he exits the room.

I like Brian Hawkes. He's been our head teacher for four years and, although we've had our differences, I like his general outlook on education. He's caring, brave and when I've seen him working with children in the classroom he really is something special.

During the afternoon session the temperature inside school is still not much above zero. My class sit huddled together on a small carpeted area by the book trolleys to maintain heat. The radiators are still only tepid but at least it's a fraction warmer here. In between different warm-up activities we sing new songs in the round, listen to stories and play word games – in fact we do anything that doesn't require too much concentration.

Half way through the afternoon Brian Hawkes enters my classroom followed by a man in a suit and tie who I assume must be the heating engineer.

My students have temporarily forgotten about the cold as they sing a new song.

"London's burning, London's burning

Fetch the engine, fetch the engine

Fire! fire! fire! fire!

Pour on water, pour on water."

Brian is taking the engineer on a tour of my classroom. They both feel the radiators, and the heating engineer jots something down in his notebook. Brian then takes the gentleman to the windows and I see them both feeling for draughts on the single glazed frames. More notes are made.

At the end of the school day we have another get-together to find out what the LEA engineer has had to say. Apparently the boiler is working effectively but to avoid these low Monday temperatures in the future, the LEA will allow the boilers to tick over on cold weekends.

"The engineer says this sort of inconvenience is highly unusual" says Brian as he gets up to go.

"Actually, its not that unusual" says Pete Bevis. "I've been teaching at this school for over twenty years and I can tell you, we suffer like this every time we have a severe cold spell."

"I endorse Pete's view" says Anne. "I too have been here for nearly twenty years, and in very cold weather the extremities of the school are impossible to work in. My view is the heating system is not working properly" she adds.

Judy starts to change her tune when she sees that the head, the deputy and all the other teachers are determined to make a stand.

"Yes!" she says. "I agree wholeheartedly with Mr Hawkes. It's no good grumbling, we must take action." And I smile because listening to Judy calling for action is like hearing the Queen demanding a republic.

"You're not one of those lefties who sell Socialist Worker, are you, Judy?" I ask, teasing."

How dare you? I read the Mail only and I'm proud of it, thank you very much" she says, and leaves for the warmth of her own home.

"Ugh!" I tink I'd sooner admit to reading Socialist Worker than the bloody Mail" scoffs Mrs O'Brien after Judy has left.

By the following Monday the temperatures are back down to almost zero inside school and the head teacher and staff are angrier than ever. However, by Thursday the school's warmed up again but the forecast for the following weekend is bleak.

I call a union meeting for lunchtime and all the teachers attend except Brian who's in the head teachers' union. The discussion is about whether we should refuse to teach in such cold conditions.

Attitudes have hardened now but there's still plenty of anxiety, as there usually is when discussing industrial action.

"I'll put my cards on the table straight away" says Judy. "Action? Yes. But not action that will hurt children's learning."

Pete Bevis then makes a telling intervention.

"Judy. None of us want to harm children's learning but don't you realise you're hurting children by doing nothing to protect them from the cold?" he says.

"No" replies Judy. "Mr Hawkes has already made our point effectively to the LEA. Therefore, I suggest we limit our union action to writing a letter to the Authority stating our collective view as classroom teachers."

This provokes a general grumbling from the group.

"The council's had twenty bloody years to put this right" says Mrs O'Brien. I tink we really have to step up the pressure on the LEA otherwise we might have to suffer for another twenty years,"

After ten more minutes of discussion I call for a vote on Judy's suggestion but it falls because no teacher is willing to second it. The other proposal is that we refuse to teach our children from Monday if the school temperatures are below the legal minimum. As there is an obvious discord amongst union members, we agree to a secret ballot.

The result is not quite what I expect: 11 votes in favour of the action, plus one vote with "abstain" scribbled on it.

When I inform our head teacher he tells me it's only what he expected.

The next day, Friday, I hand our bursar an agreed letter regarding the union's position which may be used to send out to parents.

It reads:

Dear Parents/Carers,

Members of the National Union of Teachers at St Hilda's Junior School, voted yesterday to take industrial action. We plan to refuse to teach children from 9am Monday morning, for one day, unless classroom temperatures reach the legal minimum.

This is not a decision we take lightly and we apologise if this cause problems for parents, especially those who have to go out to work.

However, we feel it is time to make a stand to ensure no child or teacher suffers from the cold while learning at our school.

Therefore, there is a possibility that come Monday, children will be walked home from school by staff members, and so we ask you to make appropriate child-care arrangements.

Yours sincerely,

Brian Hawkes incorporates my letter in an official message that goes home to all parents on Friday evening.

By Monday morning the classroom temperatures are once again way below the legal requirement and less than half the children turn up for school.

Those who do, are put into groups of ten depending on where they live and an adult is assigned to walk them home or to carers.

The head teacher hurriedly organises an in-service training day in the school staffroom. With the use of mobile oil-radiators the room is made to feel quite snug.

By ten o'clock there are three council vans parked up and about half a dozen heating engineers on the job. By one o'clock in the afternoon new pumps have been installed in the central heating system and the radiators in the farthest classrooms are hot enough to fry an egg on.

The room temperatures are still well below what they should be but it's clear that the problem has been solved once and for all. That evening, Radio Sheffield and Dearne Radio announce that the school will be open as usual for pupils the following day.

By two o'clock on Tuesday afternoon the radiators are working so well, teachers in the two end classrooms have to open windows to let in a bit of cold air.

What a pity that it took two decades before a minor fault in the heating system was acknowledged and corrected; and how wrong is it that we teachers had to close the school for pupils in order to get this done?

Interestingly, despite the inconvenience to parents and carers, the school receives not one complaint regarding the school closure.

The teachers are delighted with our success and spread the word to all NUT Union reps in the Barnsley area. However, Judy thinks differently and makes it known that she believes the Authority probably intended to correct the faulty heating system, all along.

However, no one else shares her opinion.

A BLUE PLAQUE BRIAN GLOVER

In 2022, on the 25th anniversary of Brian's death, I decide to launch a campaign to get Brian Glover a well-deserved blue plaque.

I contact my Kes colleagues to gauge their interest but although they all agree with the general sentiment, none of them are able to commit to another time-consuming project. The Barry Hines statue project was thrilling but draining.

So that leaves my partner, Janet Richardson, and when she sees how passionate I feel about it, she agrees to become our second committee member. I feel hugely relieved because I really value her opinion.

My first move is to expand the group, so I post several messages on Facebook and in the Barnsley Chronicle. They detail our aims, ask for volunteers to join us and also appeals for help in tracing Brian's first wife, Elaine and daughter, Maxine.

The response we get is mixed. I'm elated that three of Brian's former pupils from Longcar Central and Racecommon Road, agree to join us. They are: Lynn Manterfield, Alan Earp and my best mate from Longcar, Ged Wilcock. Both Alan and Ged's wives (Karen and Barbara) are also happy to help with decision-making and problem-solving. However, I still have no luck in tracing Brian's first family.

Then I get a welcome Facebook message from John Love of the Barnsley Civic Trust because he's heard about our project in the Chronicle and wants to help.

First of all, John is rightly concerned about whether we can actually raise the £300 necessary to purchase the plaque. However, when I tell him that I headed the Kes Statue project which finished up raising nearly £90k, he's convinced.

My hopes are also raised over tracing the Glover family, when a woman tells me she's a relative and agrees to pass on my details. Sadly, nothing materialises. I know I should also try to contact Brian's second family who live in London but what's the chance of success there, when I can't even link up with his first family in my home town?

I discuss the problem with the group and we agree to go ahead with the project regardless, otherwise we could be waiting for ever.

Technology is not really my thing, but somehow I miraculously set up an internet fund-raiser and the money begins to roll in. Furthermore, money is also sent to me directly through cash, cheques and bank transfer, and it soon becomes clear that Brian Glover is still an extremely popular figure.

Next thing to consider is where to place the plaque. We need somewhere in the town centre where it can be seen by as many people as possible, but which Brian had some association with. Eventually, we come up with three possible places: the Civic Hall where he regularly wrestled professionally; the residential flats which have replaced the Junction Gymnasium where Brian trained; and Chennells Bar where he was filmed making a documentary eulogising his beloved Barnsley.

The Civic seems the most appropriate place and there's already a blue plaque fixed to it in honour of the late Barnsley comedian, Charlie Williams. Unfortunately, the town planner's response is a definite no. They're adamant they do NOT want a blue plaque on what is a listed building and they say the Charlie William's plaque was attached without permission.

Chennells Bar becomes our second choice because it's bang in the centre of town where there's a large footfall - whereas, the Junction Flats don't match these requirements.

The Landlord, Craig Bristoe, puts me in touch with Mark Wass, who represents the owners, Amber Taverns. They're not only keen on the idea, they're also eager to offer financial support.

As our experiences with the Kes Statue project has made us more knowledgeable about organising events like this, we decide on Thursday 22nd September, at noon, for the blue plaque to be unveiled. That will give our project, maximum media coverage.

By mid July, I finally make contact with Brian's first family. His ex wife, Elaine, is lukewarm about the blue plaque idea but her daughter, Maxine, is more supportive.

Maxine helps us make contact with Brian's second wife, Tara Prem, and their son Gus. They email me, so we're now in touch with everyone who matters.

By late July, we've already made over £600 of the £1,500 needed, when I get a message from the Barnsley artist, Neil Richardson.

He proposes to paint a picture of Brian, make a limited edition of 40 prints and sell them at £25 each. After deducting costs our group could make quite a sum.

Neil also enlists the support of Ian Langworthy, a local business man, who's willing to sell the mounted prints for us from his Casual's Cafe on Doncaster Road, for no charge.

However, the biggest coup of all is persuading one of the most respected film-makers in the world to jointly undertake the unveiling.

Ken Loach chose Brian Glover for the part of Mr Sugden in the film, Kes, in 1968 and Brian's performance helped turn the film into a phenomenal success.

Ken lives in Bath and at the age of 86 it's too much to expect him to come all the way up north to Barnsley for the third time in three years. Nevertheless, I explain to him in an email that if I didn't invite him and he was upset about this, I'd never forgive myself.

Fortunately, Ken Jumps at the chance of jointly unveiling the plaque.

Three other speakers have also accepted invitations: The actor, Dai Bradley, who played Billy Casper in the film Kes; Barnsley's Mayor, Councillor Sarah Tattersall; and Joe Rollin from the Orgreave Truth and Justice campaign.

Joe is invited because Brian was also a well-known socialist. He appeared several times as the voice of the political left on BBCs Question Time and also gave generously to the striking miners' Xmas Fund during the '84/'85 industrial dispute.

We know the decision to invite Joe might prove controversial but we're determined not to have Brian's character sanitised for political ends.

We're also aware that Brian was a dyed-in-the-wool republican. However, since many royalists are still in mourning over the death of Queen Elizabeth we think it disrespectful to focus on this.

A short while before the unveiling day, Dawn Wright, a lecturer at Barnsley College, whom I've known for 30 years, messages me to ask if she could invite Ken up to the College in the afternoon of the 22nd. She wants him to speak to a large group of her students about the film, Kes.

"If it's okay with Ken" I tell her, "then it's okay with me." When Ken receives his request from Dawn, his PA, Emma, seeks my consent first and then happily agrees to it.

Now everything's in place for a grand celebration of Brian's life: We have the Old Blowers Brass Band performing for us in Peel Square and a list of outstanding speakers lined up. Moreover, there's a buffet organised by the Chennell's landlord; some media guarantees that they will attend and hundreds of Brian Glover fans eager for the day to arrive.

All we need now is for the sun to shine down on us.

On the eve of the big day, Andy Birks – Janet's son - uses his professional joinery skills to fix the blue plaque to the wall outside Chennells. It's then covered temporarily with cardboard.

Next morning, the sun does indeed shine on us in all its glory.

Pete Deakin - from the *Kes is Coming Home* group – is helping me remove the cardboard and covering the plaque with the shiny veil material and gold cord. It's really awkward but Pete manages a way through the problems. As we complete the task, Peel Square is beginning to fill with people and we can hear the brass band warming up.

Matt Mitchell, events manager with Barnsley Council, has done a magnificent job in organising a big marquee to protect the musicians in the event of rain. Furthermore, he's provided us with 30-odd chairs and an excellent public address system.

All the Kes Group, who worked so hard to make our Barry Hines statue project so successful, are also present, and roll their sleeves up to lend a valuable hand. My partner, Janet, and Lynn Manterfield are organising everything in the pub and Alan Earp is on duty, making sure no one spoils the occasion by unveiling the plaque prematurely.

By 11:45 the Square has dozens of TV and newspaper journalists milling around but I'm mainly interested in ensuring our own media volunteers - Paul Hilton, Dave Cherry and Dave Simmons - are given prime positions.

As I introduce the speakers I notice, in the crowd, two very famous actors, Philip Jackson and Dave Hill. They were very close friends of Brian and have come to join in the celebrations.

The band and all the speeches are thoroughly enjoyed by the crowd and then they migrate en masse, 30 metres, to Wellington Street for the actual unveiling ceremony.

After the countdown and three cheers, the plaque is revealed by Gus Glover and Ken Loach and everyone is euphoric.

As the celebrities are button-holed by the media and fans for interviews, autographs and selfies, scores of supporters enter the pub for the buffet and a pint. In one corner of the pub, Alan Jones and five other accomplished musicians are playing lively, instrumental music.

At 1:50 pm, Dawn Wright, Dai Bradley (and his partner) plus Paul Hilton and myself, escort Ken the 150 metres to Barnsley College for an hour of being quizzed by about 150 students.

Everyone appreciates this and Ken Loach is enjoying it so much he over-runs by 10 minutes.

When it's over, I entrust Ken's safe-keeping into the hands of Pete Deakin and nip back down to Chennell's to say good bye to Tara, Gus, Philip Jackson, Dave Hill and their respective partners.

Philip insists on a group photo.

As they finally depart for home we all shake hands, and Gus Glover says to me:

"We're all really grateful for everything you've done for my dad, Ronnie, but I just wish you'd re-consider and build a statue for him."

Gus must see my eyes light up. Creating a statue of Brian Glover in the precinct, with a football under his arm, is a dream I've harboured secretly for nine months.

Therefore, I look Gus Glover straight in the eye and say to him, cryptically:

"Wait and see, Gus. You never know."

And I start to wonder whether I'll ever get the chance to write a third volume of Barnsley stories, titled: *'Building A Statue for Brian Glover'*.

Hmmm.

Left to right: Philip Jackson, Ronnie Steele, Gus Glover, Dave Hill and Tara Prem.

THE FINALE: LEON ARRAS THE MAN FROM PARIS

Finally, I want to finish this book in the same way that I started it – with a short tale about Brian Glover the wrestler, by Eva Edgar:

"I remember watching Leon Arras at the Civic and this woman, sat at the side of me, was wholeheartedly backing the 'Frenchman'.

She got to her feet screaming for Leon to pull his opponent's hair. But as she did, she unconsciously grabbed two fists-full of hair of the man sat in front and shook him like a dog shakes a rag doll.

Fortunately, the poor man saw the funny side of it and we all had a good laugh.

Yes, I knew all along that Leon Arras was really Brian Glover. I lived only 30 yards from him.

Smashing bloke!